"God has uniquely blessed Br[...] deepest needs of our generation. He has preached them from his pulpit, lived them in his life, and written them in this wonderful book. Read it and celebrate. I did."

— JEANNETTE CLIFT GEORGE, actress, playwright, producer

"John Bisagno gives us the encouraging word of an accomplished pastor who has been there. Every believer needs a copy of this book on their nightstand for a Monday-morning rescue and resuscitation."

— MAC BRUNSON, senior pastor, First Baptist Church, Jacksonville, Florida

"John Bisagno is one of the truly outstanding Christian leaders of our day. I heartily recommend *Wisdom for Life* to anyone who wants to live a fuller, more faithful, and more satisfying life. You'll love it!"

— DR. STEVE WENDE, senior pastor, First Methodist Church, Houston

WISDOM for LIFE

Keys to Finishing Well

DR. JOHN BISAGNO

NAVPRESS

Discipleship Inside Out™

NavPress is the publishing ministry of The Navigators, an international Christian organization and leader in personal spiritual development. NavPress is committed to helping people grow spiritually and enjoy lives of meaning and hope through personal and group resources that are biblically rooted, culturally relevant, and highly practical.

**For a free catalog go to www.NavPress.com
or call 1.800.366.7788 in the United States or 1.800.839.4769 in Canada.**

ISBN-13: 978-1-61747-180-3

Cover design by Arvid Wallen
Cover image by Robert Ladkowski, Shutterstock

Some of the anecdotal illustrations in this book are true to life and are included with the permission of the persons involved. All other illustrations are composites of real situations, and any resemblance to people living or dead is coincidental.

Unless otherwise identified, all Scripture quotations in this publication are taken from the King James Version (KJV). Other versions used include: the *Holy Bible, New International Version®* (NIV®), Copyright © 1973, 1978, 1984 by International Bible Society, used by permission of Zondervan, all rights reserved; the *Holy Bible,* New Living Translation (NLT), copyright © 1996, 2004. Used by permission of Tyndale House Publishers, Inc., Wheaton, Illinois 60189. All rights reserved; the New King James Version (NKJV). Copyright © 1982 by Thomas Nelson, Inc. Used by permission. All rights reserved; the New American Standard Bible® (NASB), Copyright © 1960, 1962, 1963, 1968, 1971, 1972, 1973, 1975, 1977, 1995 by The Lockman Foundation. Used by permission; *THE MESSAGE* (MSG). Copyright © 1993, 1994, 1995, 1996, 2000, 2001, 2002. Used by permission of NavPress Publishing Group; *The Living Bible* (TLB), copyright © 1971, used by permission of Tyndale House Publishers, Inc., Wheaton, IL 60189, all rights reserved; and the Holman Christian Standard Bible (HCSB)® Copyright © 2003, 2002, 2000, 1999 by Holman Bible Publishers. All rights reserved.

Bisagno, John R.
  Wisdom for life : keys to finishing well / John R. Bisagno.
      p. cm.
  Includes bibliographical references (p.   ).
  ISBN 978-1-61747-180-3
  1. Christian life—Baptist authors.   I. Title.
  BV4501.3.B498 2012
  248.4'86—dc23

                                                                2011024909

Printed in the United States of America

1 2 3 4 5 6 7 8 / 16 15 14 13 12

CONTENTS

FOREWORD

Books abound on how we are to faithfully and effectively live our lives as Christians. The challenge with so many good spiritual resources at our disposal is our limited capacity to absorb this material in a way that is easy to assimilate and use for our daily lives. The stresses and strains of daily life have increased the challenge of finding the most efficient means of accessing spiritual input that helps us live effective lives on earth while simultaneously preparing us for heaven.

This is why *Wisdom for Life*, by my friend John Bisagno, is such a special book. It uniquely capsulizes the key areas of wise living in easily digestible, bite-size summaries, which allows the reader to understand and utilize the biblical principles that it exposes. Each week, for a whole year, you will receive an impactful spiritual nugget that will help foster spiritual health in your life. Each "key" will unlock a door, gaining you access to one of God's foundational principles for pursuing a life well lived.

No matter what your spiritual level currently is, this extraordinary work will guide you to the next spiritual level as you meditate on and walk in the light of its truth.

Since the essence of wisdom is the application of biblical truth to life's everyday realities, by the time you finish this work, your life's key chain will be full of all you need to progress as a visible verbal follower of

Christ who has learned to live life wisely. And when this life ends, you will be able to transition to eternity knowing that you finished well in time.

DR. TONY EVANS
founder and senior pastor,
Oak Cliff Bible Fellowship, Dallas, Texas;
founder and president, The Urban Initiative

INTRODUCTION

God's extraordinary people don't set out to be that way. Being special is not on their radar. At the heart and soul of their very being is that He is special, and they just love Him and want to honor Him.

In the process, they become more like the Master and make it all the way to the finish line.

And it's relatively simple. It's not doing the grandiose, not performing the spectacular; it's the little things, the everyday way-of-life things—step by step, day by day—that make the journey sweet. And special.

I have been blessed to know special people in many walks of life. University presidents and professional athletes, mega pastors and congressmen, as well as gardeners, carpenters, and sales clerks have blessed my life. Really blessed my life. Each did the ordinary things very well—every day—all the way.

Here is a year's supply of spiritual vitamins—tiny pearls I have seen produce very big results in the lives of some of God's best children.

Take one each weekend with a glass of Living Water, read it over three or four times, think about it for a week, and let it energize you all the way to the finish line.

Ready!

Set!

Celebrate!

This is what the LORD *says:*
"*The wise must not boast in his wisdom;*
the mighty must not boast in his might;
the rich must not boast in his riches.
But the one who boasts should boast in this,
that he understands and knows Me—
that I am the LORD*, showing faithful love,*
justice, and righteousness on the earth,
for I delight in these things."
This is the LORD'*s declaration.*
JEREMIAH 9:23-24 (HCSB)

CHAPTER 1

LOVE THE TRUTH

S in always takes you farther than you want to go. Keeps you longer than you want to stay. Costs you more than you expect to pay.

"You are the man!" (2 Samuel 12:7, NKJV). With these words, the prophet Nathan confronted King David about his adultery with Bathsheba and his murder of Uriah, her husband.

With David's response, everything was on the line. David stood condemned before the bar of truth. He was indeed *the man*. He had premeditatedly plotted and perpetrated adultery with Bathsheba, and the price tag would be brutal.

How would David respond to the truth? Heaven held its breath. Angels strained to hear David's response to Nathan's charges. He could say anything. He could do anything. He was supreme potentate of the kingdom.

He could have simply abrogated the law. Lesser leaders have declared themselves above the law. David could have said, "I therefore decree that adultery is no longer a sin—stealing a man's wife, no longer a crime." He could have annihilated Nathan. He could have executed the prophet. He could at least have fired him and hired a new court chaplain.

Admitting truth would cost David and cost him dearly, and indeed it did.

But there was one thing more important to David than David, and that was *the truth*. Let David pay. God's truth had been spoken, and God's truth must stand at any cost.

Let David suffer.

Let truth be exalted.

"So David said to Nathan, '*I have sinned* against the LORD.' And Nathan said to David, 'The LORD also has put away your sin; you shall not die'" (2 Samuel 12:13, NKJV, emphasis added). David's forgiveness was automatic upon his confession.

Do you realize how important truth is to God? Pilate questioned Jesus perhaps for hours and philosophically asked, "What is truth?" (John 18:38).

Jesus spoke not a word. By His silence, He spoke volumes: "Pilate, you have examined Me for hours, and although trained in the finest disciplines of the Roman judiciary, you are asking Me, 'What is truth?' For the last two hours you've been looking at the truth. If you don't know it when you see it, you wouldn't understand it if I tried to explain it to you."

In John 14:6 Jesus said He was THE truth. That little three-letter word speaks of exclusivity, the *only* truth, and specificity, *precisely* the truth. "I am the way, the truth, and the life: no man cometh unto the Father, but by me."

Satan is *the lie*. Jesus is *the truth*. If you would follow Him who is *the truth*, you must walk in truth. When Nathan confronted David, David admitted his sin—in truth. God accepted his repentance and said, "I have found David . . . a man after my own heart" (Acts 13:22, NIV). So thorough was David's repentance that God used him as an example to his son, Solomon.

As for you, if you walk before Me as your father David walked, and do according to all that I have commended you, and if you keep My statutes and My judgments, then I will establish the throne of your kingdom, as I covenanted with David your father, saying, "You shall not fail to have a man as ruler in Israel." (2 Chronicles 7:17-18, NKJV, emphasis added)

David was a great sinner, but he also was a great repenter. Psalm 51 is the gold standard for the truly penitent. God used David's brokenness over his sin to make of him the great king he would become.

The prophet Nathan saw what David *was*. God saw what he *could become* if he embraced truth.

Jesus was pleased to call Himself the Son of David. No wonder they call it amazing grace!

David, a man after God's own heart, was a lover of truth. Are you? If you aren't walking in truth, do something about it now. If you can't be that kind of person, it's over before you start.

I have no greater joy than this, to hear of my children walking in the truth.

3 JOHN 4 (NASB)

CHAPTER 2

MAINTAIN BALANCE

True wisdom has a special sense of balance.

Moses knew when to wait quietly in the desert and when to challenge Pharaoh. David was both a king and a prophet. Elijah knew when to confront the prophets of Baal on Mount Carmel and when to wait quietly by the brook Cherith. Jesus tenderly restored an embarrassed adulteress one day and drove the moneychangers from the temple the next.

Satan tempted Jesus to jump from the pinnacle of the temple and destroy Himself. Predictably he quoted a half-truth out of context:

> *It is written, He shall give his angels charge concerning thee: and in their hands they shall bear thee up, lest at any time thou dash thy foot against a stone.*
>
> *Jesus said unto him, It is written again, Thou shalt not tempt the Lord thy God.* (Matthew 4:6-7)

Balance is also found in the great truths of the Bible. Paul said, "By grace are ye saved through faith" (Ephesians 2:8). James said, "Faith, if it has no works, is dead" (James 2:17, NASB). Faith not validated by fruitful evidence is not saving faith.

The humanity of Jesus must be balanced with the deity of Jesus. Humanity without deity is pure liberalism.

Deity without humanity is Gnosticism. The Gnostics taught that what appeared to be the body of Jesus was an aberration of the mind. No body, no blood. No blood, no salvation.

Billy Graham preached both the love of God and the judgment of God, with a sensitive balance of compassion and conviction. You can't be so positive, you are never negative; so encouraging, you're never warning. Sometimes the best love is tough love.

Like Old and New Testament, husband and wife, or freedom and discipline, balance always leads to strength as one complements the other.

A pastor may comfort a widow at a graveside on Saturday and may have to confront someone on Sunday. We raised our sons with tough love. Sometimes it hurt, but today they are fine Christian men.

Balance starts with God. His love and judgment are always in view. His patience and end of patience are ever His way.

We would do well to seek the same.

A judge sentencing a young man to ten years in prison asked, "How could you go so far astray? I knew your father, a famous author, very well. He was a very successful man." The boy replied, "He never paid any attention to me; it was always those blasted books."

Balancing time between career and family can be at once delicate and difficult. Not doing it right can be devastating and deadly.

I know how to get along with humble means,
and I also know how to live in prosperity;
in any and every circumstance I have learned
the secret of being filled and going hungry,
both of having abundance and suffering need.
Philippians 4:12 (nasb)

CHAPTER 3

PASSIONATELY PERSEVERE

On October 13, 2010, the world cheered as the last of thirty-three trapped Chilean miners emerged from a shaft, drilled a quarter mile through solid rock by rescuers who would not be deterred. Heaven must have smiled. For thirty-three years our Lord was tempted in all things, endured, and lived without sin "that we may obtain mercy, and find grace to help in time of need" (Hebrews 4:16).

Jesus made it clear: "In the world you will have tribulation." But while that's the fact of the matter, it's not the end of the story. "But be of good cheer; I have *overcome* the world" (John 16:33, NKJV, emphasis added). In His power, His children are overcomers as well.

What God has called you to do is not about quitting, but about overcoming. It's not about running *away* but about running *for* the prize—honoring your high calling, fighting the good fight, not throwing in the towel in round seven. And wherever you serve—and we all do—you are called to be a winner, and winners don't quit. It's not about how easy it is. If He called you to do a specific task, then He called you to finish it.

Finishing strong is a nonnegotiable for those who follow in the Master's footsteps. He hung on the cross—for six hours—for you. Until He could say, "It is finished." Notice He didn't say *He* was finished, but *it* was finished. It was not the cry of the conquered but the Conqueror.

In the garden Jesus prayed,

Right now I am storm-tossed. And what am I going to say? "Father, get me out of this"? No, this is why I came in the first place. I'll say, "Father, put your glory on display."

A voice came out of the sky: "I have glorified it, and I'll glorify it again." (John 12:27, MSG)

Winners don't cut and run. Winners don't give up. Winners don't quit.

Vince Lombardi is the unquestioned greatest football coach who ever walked the sidelines. Mr. Lombardi got it right. Who could forget his famous quote, "When the going gets tough, the tough get going"?

When you were called to run the race, you were called to finish it—no matter how tough it gets. If God wanted a quitter, He would have called a quitter, but He didn't—He called you.

Just do it!

Quit? Don't even think about it!

God's people are winners. And winners never quit and quitters never win. Keep going, keep fighting, keep serving. Win. Just do it.

- Tim LaHaye is still preaching at age 83.
- Marge Caldwell conducted women's conferences until she was 86.
- Dalton Havard is 86 and still preaching.
- Christian playwright and actress Jeannette Clift George is going stronger than ever at 86.
- Mother Teresa ministered in the slums of India until her death at 86.
- Famed philanthropist J. C. Penney served until 96.
- George Beverly Shea still sings the gospel at 102.
- Noah preached 120 years.
- Moses served until he was 120.

- Isaac served until he was 140.
- Abraham served until he was 145.

When things get tough, and they will, remember that His grace is sufficient. More than sufficient for everything.

"The temptations in your life are no different from what others experience. And God is faithful. He will not allow the temptation to be more than you can stand. When you are tempted, he will show you a way out so that you can endure" (1 Corinthians 10:13, NLT). The expression "a way out" means "out of failure" in the midst of the trial, victory through His all-sufficient grace.

God inspired this verse.

Paul experienced it.

Together they wrote it.

No one ever had greater reason to quit than Paul. But he didn't. He wrote,

> *Are they ministers of Christ?—I speak as a fool—I am more: in labors more abundant, in stripes above measure, in prisons more frequently, in deaths often. From the Jews five times I received forty stripes minus one. Three times I was beaten with rods; once I was stoned; three times I was shipwrecked; a night and a day I have been in the deep; in journeys often, in perils of waters, in perils of robbers, in perils of my own countrymen, in perils of the Gentiles, in perils in the city, in perils in the wilderness, in perils in the sea, in perils among false brethren; in weariness and toil, in sleeplessness often, in hunger and thirst, in fastings often, in cold and nakedness—besides the other things, what comes upon me daily: my deep concern for all the churches.* (2 Corinthians 11:23-28, NKJV)

Paul found God's grace sufficient and His smile worth the price. And so can you.

I have fought the good fight, I have finished the course,
I have kept the faith; in the future there is laid up for me
the crown of righteousness, which the Lord, the righteous
Judge, will award to me on that day; and not only to me,
but also to all who have loved His appearing.

2 TIMOTHY 4:7-8 (NASB)

CHAPTER 4

THOROUGHLY PREPARE

God's Word is the heart and soul of the man or woman prepared to run the race—and win.

No coach allows his team to take the field until they first know the strengths and weaknesses of the other team. Day and night, team members study to make sure they know the exact angles the other team will take and how to attack them. We need a good plan of attack. "All Scripture is inspired by God and profitable for teaching, for reproof, for correction, for training in righteousness; so that the man of God may be adequate, equipped for every good work" (2 Timothy 3:16-17, NASB).

It can take longer to draw plans for a house than to build the house. During the five years of relocating our church, the planning stage took three years, the construction only two.

Only 10 percent of an army actually fights the battle; 90 percent plan and provide for them.

Moses spent forty years in the wilderness before he led the children of Israel from bondage to the Promised Land.

Paul went to Arabia for three years before he preached a sermon or wrote an epistle.

Jesus prepared thirty years for a three-year ministry. Today people who are going into full-time ministry go to seminary and prepare three years for a thirty-year ministry. What a difference!

If we want to finish well, we must be thoroughly prepared for every good work. Good work in ministry or anywhere in life is not trumped up at the last minute. It is characterized by thorough planning, good preparation, and thoughtful deliberation.

Sitting in the Oakland International Airport, I watched as a group of passengers stepped off the plane from Hawaii. Most were clad in shorts, tank tops, and flip-flops. What they did not know was that the temperature that day in Oakland was 39 degrees. As they walked off the plane to retrieve their bags, I thought, *How many of them don't know and how many just don't care?* It's important to care enough to prepare.

My sermon preparation is always done from a perspective that's a bit unusual. I begin with the assumption that no one will agree with my proposition. When you're asked to do something important, be it a political speech or a Sunday school lesson, put yourself in the shoes of a potential naysayer. Begin with the assumption that no one will agree with your proposition.

Think like the detractor. What will be the question? Or the argument? Wherein will the debate lie? In what form will the antagonist respond? Preclude, anticipate, prepare, and present your case thoroughly furnished.

Are you ready? Really ready?

"Always be ready to give a defense to everyone who asks you a reason for the hope that is in you, with meekness and fear" (1 Peter 3:15, NKJV). That's how lawyers go to trial, both prosecutors and defenders. They prepare thoroughly. They've done their homework. They're ready.

The apologetic, the argument, the logic, the reason, the defense—these are the missing ingredients in too many sermons today and in too many situations in the church with both pastor and layperson. We give too little thought to how we will answer the fair and simple question, "Why?"

You can be a mile wide and an inch deep when it comes to preparation. Major on the mile deep, and the inch wide will become a mile.

Take care of the depth of your life, and God will take care of the breadth of your life. Every discussion, every lesson, every meeting, every business presentation, every family issue deserves thorough preparation. Be fully prepared, thoroughly furnished for every opportunity and every challenge. Our Lord and those whose lives we touch deserve no less.

Rome wasn't built in a day, and neither are great lives.

Is there anyone here who, planning to build a new
house, doesn't first sit down and figure the cost?
LUKE 14:28 (MSG)

CHAPTER 5

KEEP YOUR COMPOSURE

NFL Hall of Famer Roger Staubach, a great Christian, is legendary for his composure under pressure. One Sunday afternoon just before a make-or-break play, they measured his pulse rate "in the pocket" at a cool sixty.

Composure. We hear it in the pilot's voice in the midst of turbulence, and we sense it in the spirit of God's choicest servants. It's always there. We can't make good decisions any other way.

Perhaps that's why in the Shepherd's Psalm (Psalm 23), David talks about walking — not running, struggling, or hurrying — through the valley of the shadow of death. "The valley of the shadow of death" (verse 4) is a literal valley a few miles outside of Jerusalem in the wilderness of Judea. At the bottom of the valley are green pastures and fresh water. The sides of the valley are crisscrossed with dozens of narrow, dangerous sheep trails. The sheep have to get to the water and grass on the floor of the valley, but they are clumsy and some fall off and are lost.

Through the years, the shepherds became fatalistic. They reasoned, "The less time we're in the valley, the less sheep we'll lose." They *ran* the sheep over the trails, rushing them through the valley as quickly as possible. David was saying, "Time out! The Lord is my Shepherd. He holds my hand. I don't have to play games, and I don't have to live in denial. I don't have to psych myself out, run through the valley, and get it over with as soon as possible. With dignity, peace, and composure, I can *walk* through the valley of the shadow of death."

But peace under pressure, composure in a crisis, is not something you grip your knuckles, or twist up your face, and get. It's real, and it's real because it comes from God. Psalm 51 probes the depth of David's stress. Unimaginable! Unfathomable! I don't know whether someone rearranged the order along the way, but I think the calm of the Twenty-Third Psalm must surely have come after the turbulence of the Fifty-First Psalm.

The only reason we don't get rattled in the valley of difficulty and stress is because "The LORD is my shepherd" (Psalm 23:1), *really* my Shepherd.

Walking calmly through the valley—or on the mountaintop—is a nonnegotiable character trait for those who want to finish well. Lose your calm spirit under stress and lose respect. Lose respect and lose your influence. Lose your influence and lose it all.

The truth is we can't control ourselves; we can only yield ourselves to the Spirit of Christ who gives us self-control. Coolness under pressure is a gift of God and the fruit of His indwelling Spirit.

Your attitude in response to pressure is a hundred times more important than *whatever issue is causing the pressure*. Long after they forget the issue, people will remember your sweet spirit, or lack of it. One short sentence, spoken in anger with one small bodily instrument called the tongue, can equate to one invalidated testimony. You can indeed catch more flies with honey. "But the fruit of the Spirit is love, joy, peace, longsuffering, gentleness, goodness, faith, meekness, temperance" (Galatians 5:22-23).

Years ago a man wrote me the most caustic letter I have ever received. I wanted to eat him alive, but instead I kept my composure, waited two weeks, and sent a kind letter in response. I expressed my love and interest in his family and assured him of my prayers for God's best in their lives. Today they are active members of our church.

Rudyard Kipling's immortal *If* sums it up:

If you can keep your head when all about you
Are losing theirs and blaming it on you;
If you can trust yourself when all men doubt you,
But make allowance for their doubting too;
If you can wait and not be tired by waiting,
Or being lied about, don't deal in lies,
Or being hated don't give way to hating,
And yet don't look too good, nor talk too wise;

If you can dream — and not make dreams your master;
If you can think — and not make thoughts your aim,
If you can meet with Triumph and Disaster
And treat those two impostors just the same;
If you can bear to hear the truth you've spoken
Twisted by knaves to make a trap for fools,
Or watch the things you gave your life to, broken,
And stoop and build 'em up with worn-out tools;

If you can make one heap of all your winnings
And risk it on one turn of pitch-and-toss,
And lose, and start again at your beginnings
And never breathe a word about your loss;
If you can force your heart and nerve and sinew
To serve your turn long after they are gone,
And so hold on when there is nothing in you
Except the Will which says to them: "Hold on!"

If you can talk with crowds and keep your virtue,
Or walk with Kings — nor lose the common touch,
If neither foes nor loving friends can hurt you,
If all men count with you, but none too much;
If you can fill the unforgiving minute
With sixty seconds' worth of distance run,
Yours is the Earth and everything that's in it,
And — which is more — you'll be a Man, my son![1]

We work hard with our own hands. When we are cursed,
we bless: when we are persecuted, we endure it.

1 Corinthians 4:12 (niv)

CHAPTER 6

BE A FRIEND

Jackie Robinson was the first African American to play Major League Baseball. Breaking baseball's color barrier, he faced jeering crowds in virtually every stadium. One day while playing in his home stadium in Brooklyn, he committed an error. The crowd began to boo him. He stood at second base, humiliated as the fans jeered. Shortstop Pee Wee Reese came over and stood next to him. He put his arm around Jackie Robinson and faced the crowd. The fans grew quiet.

How do you treat people? If your answer is not *all alike*, then your answer is *all wrong*. Favoritism, self-serving friendship, is the death knell of Christian testimony. People will spot you as a self-serving phony in a New York minute.

David was an exceptional man, a man after God's own heart. One might easily overlook a quiet insight into his life that's buried in an obscure passage in 2 Samuel 9.

One day King David was thinking of Jonathan, the great friend of his youth, and asked, "Is there anyone still left of the house of Saul to whom I can show kindness for Jonathan's sake?" (verse 1, NIV). The answer came back, "There is still a son of Jonathan; he is crippled in both feet" (verse 3, NIV). David had him brought to the palace, restored unto him his father's land, and fed him at the king's table the rest of his life.

David loved his friends. Not just the kings and queens, as do the self-serving. He loved the great and small. If you were a friend of David's, you were a friend for life. Just a small story, only a few verses that barely made The Book, but it made a huge impression on God, who said, "I have found David . . . a man after my own heart" (Acts 13:22, NIV).

A friend is the one who comes in when the whole world has gone out.

Jesus' exceptional servants follow in His footsteps. To be like Christ means never losing the common touch. Selective friendship and spiritual integrity are by definition mutually exclusive. Never was it better said, "Jesus, what a friend of sinners." Our Lord loves everyone and loves each equally, as do those who walk in His footsteps.

You can't be a friend of God and not be a friend to all people. That includes everyone, great and small.

I no longer call you servants, because a servant does not know his master's business. Instead, I have called you friends.

JOHN 15:15 (NIV)

CHAPTER 7

SEEK BROKENNESS

M ost of us can relate to the low point in the life of Simon Peter.
"Then Peter remembered the word Jesus had spoken: 'Before the
rooster crows, you will disown me three times.' And he went outside and
wept bitterly" (Matthew 26:75, NIV).

We see so much of ourselves in Peter—always the pop off, always
the first to speak, always *the man*. He fell from Peter "the rock" to Peter
the "I know not the man."

Peter's confession, "Thou art the Christ" (Matthew 16:16), and
Jesus' pronouncement, "And upon this rock I will build my church"
(verse 18), are at once the high point of Peter's life and the low point of
Roman Catholic doctrine. Jesus' word "Peter" is the Greek word *petros*, a
small rock—a person of male gender. His word "rock" is the Greek word
petra and has no gender. It is not someone, but something.

The rock Christ was referring to was not the *humanity of Peter* but
the *deity of Jesus* that Peter had just confessed.

Peter was not the rock of the church; he was the key to world evangelism, starting at Pentecost. Jesus gave Peter the keys to the kingdom, and
Peter used them not to open the door to heaven but to open the door of
the gospel to the world—to the Jews in Acts 2 and the Gentiles in Acts
10, when he preached the gospel in their hearing for the first time.

But before Jesus' promise to Peter and its fulfillment *in* Peter, something had to happen *to* Peter.

29

After Peter denied knowing Christ, "he went out, and wept bitterly" (Matthew 26:75). Before his denial, Peter was a bit of a braggart. After his denial, he was broken, humble, and usable.

Broken vessels can be remade into the image of their maker: beautiful and usable. With the joy of childbirth, the pain is quickly forgotten. On Easter Sunday morning, the sorrow of Good Friday turned to beauty and life.

Before success, sorrow.

Before leadership, loss.

Before blessing, brokenness.

Not surprisingly, we neither easily nor willingly choose brokenness. It's not comfortable, but it is *necessary*. The apostle Paul wrote, "And those who are Christ's have crucified the flesh with its passions and desires" (Galatians 5:24, NKJV).

Jesus said, "He that is greatest among you shall be your servant" (Matthew 23:11). God's greatest servants have risen from the humblest of beginnings. Not until we know we are unworthy of serving are we ready to lead. Kingdom work is not something you *want* to do; it is something you *have* to do out of gratitude for what He's done for you.

"Amazing grace, how sweet the sound, that saved a wretch like me."[2] Being the *wretch* is a precondition to receiving the grace. And receiving God's grace is a prerequisite to leading others into it.

Only when we have been broken can people relate to us. He's been there; he understands. And only then can God mold us into His image and use us.

Brokenness is the way of the Cross, and it is the way of God with His people. First Corinthians 1:26-29 says,

Remember, dear brothers and sisters, that few of you were wise in the world's eyes or powerful or wealthy when God called you. Instead, God chose things the world considers foolish in order to shame those who think they are wise. And he chose things that are powerless to shame those who are powerful. God chose things despised by the world, things counted as nothing at all, and used them to bring to nothing what the world considers important. As a result, no one can ever boast in the presence of God. (NLT)

We see too little brokenness today. We see self-made, self-important executive types and rock stars but not many broken and humble servants.

Think of Jesus who was "made . . . to be sin for us, who knew no sin" (2 Corinthians 5:21). On the city garbage dump, God turned His head: "My God, my God, why hast thou forsaken me?" (Matthew 27:46).

Jesus' brokenness was done willingly on the cross and His promise came true: "If I be lifted up from the earth, [I] will draw all men unto me" (John 12:32).

Only in our willing brokenness *for Him* can we point people *to Him*.

I have been crucified with Christ; it is no longer
I who live, but Christ lives in me; and the life which
I now live in the flesh I live by faith in the Son of God,
who loved me and gave Himself for me.
GALATIANS 2:20 (NKJV)

He must increase, but I must decrease.
JOHN 3:30

CHAPTER 8

WORK HARD

My dad was a humble man, the owner of a small poultry business. He taught me the value of hard work, a legacy for which I shall be forever grateful. Five months of the year were peak business times for our hatchery; we made it then or not at all — much like the department stores at Christmas.

Every Monday morning, from March 1 through August 1, three hundred farmers came in to get their baby chicks — ten thousand of them — and we had to be ready. Incubators emptied, trays cleaned, boxes built, compartments strawed, boxes labeled, and baby chicks categorized. That meant all hands on deck from 4:00 a.m. until 5:00 p.m. every Sunday. I was playing in a high school dance band and got home late on Saturday nights or early Sunday mornings — midnight, 1:00 a.m., or 2:00 a.m. — but it made no difference. I was at work. *On time. All day.* Beginning at 4:00 a.m. every Sunday for five months.

My dad also expected me at work after school on Tuesdays and Fridays, from 3:00 p.m. to 5:00 p.m., to help unload an eighteen-wheeler full of one-hundred-pound feed sacks. I had to deliver them to the farmers on Saturdays and help clean their hen houses, with just enough time to clean up and play for the Saturday night dances. I was a drum major, so I rehearsed with the high school marching band early Tuesdays and Thursdays, not to mention a fifty-cents-per-hour part-time job at the Sureway supermarket.

When I was in grade school, we lived in the country, three miles from my school, and I rode the bus five days a week. If I missed the bus, I walked. I knew the meaning of hard work and still do. And I love it.

We're working for Him. We're working for the only thing in life of any lasting value whatsoever. Work hard and work willingly. Winners don't ever let up.

My last two and a half years in college I drove an average of two-hundred miles round trip, five nights a week, preaching at youth revivals fourteen weeks out of each eighteen-week semester. My wife, Uldine, worked at a bank, and I had a part-time job driving a delivery truck for a florist. I carried twenty hours my final semester and graduated from college at age twenty.

In my entire ministry, I only fired three staffers—all the same day, all for the same reason. They were lazy.

I still average eight to ten hours of work a day, and I'm retired. Or so I've been told.

We don't work because we have to; we work because we want to. We work because we love Him. We work because it's changing lives! We are *co-laborers* in the *work* of the kingdom. If you work for an employer, *work* for him or her. Come early, be consistent, work hard, stay late. This country was built on hard work, and so is the kingdom of God.

It doesn't matter if your job is secular or if your job is ministry. Ultimately, you still work for the Master, so don't make excuses.

There are men who want to look like a bodybuilder but don't want to work out. There are women who want to run marathons but don't want to train. There are those who want to lose weight but don't want to diet. There are people who want money but don't want to work for it. There are those who want to win souls but never witness.

Work because how you do your job matters to Him.

Work because how you do your job reflects on Him.

Work because you love Him.

Cherish every hour and put all you have into each one. Christians who finish strong have a good work ethic. Those who *make it to the end* have learned to *work to the end*, and they do it with a song in their heart and a smile on their face.

Doing your best, working hard, is a joy! It's fun!

I have brought you glory on earth
by completing the work you gave me to do.
JOHN 17:4 (NIV)

CHAPTER 9

AWAIT GOD'S TIMING

Esther was God's woman, in God's place, in God's time. Haman had devised a plot to annihilate the Jewish people. No Jewish people meant no Messiah. No Messiah meant no Savior. No Savior meant no salvation, no forgiveness, and no hope of heaven for any of us. Esther was an important link in God's plan of redemption. God spoke to Esther through Mordecai, her uncle, saying, "For if you remain completely silent at this time, relief and deliverance will arise for the Jews from another place, but you and your father's house will perish. Yet who knows whether you have come to the kingdom for such a time as this?" (Esther 4:14, NKJV).

Faithfulness is knowing that I don't have to know; God knows. I don't have to have everything under control; God does. We only have to be His man or His woman. We only have to be available and ready when He says, "For such a time as this."

And He will say it!

People who finish well learn to await God's perfect time.

They have a special sensitivity to God's perfect schedule. Our Lord indeed specializes in timing. He's never early, He's never late, He's always right on time.

God will not be bound by the limitations of the time and space He created. They did not create Him. They do not transcend Him; He transcends them. With God there is no yesterday or tomorrow; it's always just *right now*. He is the Lord of time, and timing is His specialty.

Faithful followers understand that. They are neither impetuous nor nervous, impatient nor uncaring. They are marked by a sense of God's perfect timing, and they never push. Sometimes you can go farther faster by going slower. When to act? Not too soon, not too late. How much? Not too much, not too little. Not so loud, not so soft. Not now, not yet, give it time. Wait for His time. He's got it under control. Now!

Early in the 1970s an exceptionally popular movie about demon possession packed movie theaters across America. It was the talk of all the sociology and psychology classes at Rice University and the University of Houston. The impact was powerful and the questions unending. *The time was right.* We ran a full-page ad in the *Houston Chronicle*:

"THE EXORCIST
> What it says that's right.
>> What it says that's wrong.
>>> What it doesn't say at all."

That Sunday morning the church was packed, including three over-flow rooms. Fifty-four university students received Christ as Savior.

As the second oldest Baptist church in Texas, Houston's First was very traditional. For three years I prayed and studied whether to start an additional contemporary service. Finally God said, "Now." We planned for two hundred people. Nine hundred were in attendance. By the time I retired, nearly two thousand attended that service. Today two contemporary services have nearly six thousand in attendance, plus a third major traditional service. Too soon? Too late? When we are sensitive to Him, we are always right on time.

Sensitivity to God's timing is crucial. Walk with Him and learn His pace. Listen to Him and learn His voice. Wait on Him. See His hand.

Sense it in your soul. Now. Right now! Be careful; you may be making the right decision—at the wrong time.

Don't get in a hurry. Seven hundred years after the promise, the star shone over Bethlehem and Abraham's seed was born.

God's time is not our time, but it's always the *best* time and *on* time. If you stay close to His heart, you will sense His purpose and gladly await His perfect timing to accomplish it. Only in retrospect can you see the time was right.

Wait on the Lord. Not too fast, not too slow. Never early, never late. Always on time.

***

To everything there is a season,
a time for every purpose under heaven.
ECCLESIASTES 3:1 (NKJV)

CHAPTER 10

PURSUE WISDOM

W isdom will take you further than a PhD, good looks, a charming personality, and a $64 vocabulary. It may be a Christian's most valuable quality. "Above all and before all, do this: Get Wisdom! Write this at the top of your list: Get Understanding!" (Proverbs 4:7, MSG).

Education is important, but knowledge exceeds education. Common sense surpasses knowledge, and wisdom goes far beyond common sense. While it is often said, "Wisdom comes from experience," God's Word says, "For the LORD gives wisdom; from His mouth come knowledge and understanding" (Proverbs 2:6, NKJV). If wisdom came only from experience, every old person would be wise.

The truth is that wisdom comes by learning what God would teach us *from* the experiences of life. Wisdom is a gift of God. Knowledge comprehends the facts and understands the truth. Wisdom knows how to *apply* truth to real-life situations. Knowledge gives information. Wisdom correctly acts upon it.

When our son Tim was a freshman, he played on a small college national championship football team. But Tim didn't really care for the school. As a sophomore, they promised increased playing time if he would stay. Tim was never a quitter at anything. He's a sticker and a stayer. He also had God-given wisdom.

"To stay in a school I really don't like just because I'm not a quitter isn't a good decision," he reasoned, and he changed schools. That was wisdom.

We sold a country home in which we planned to retire. One day Uldine had said, "You know, the anticipation of going up there each week is more enjoyable than actually being there." That was wisdom. We sold it. And we're glad.

Another time we considered buying a home we weren't crazy about because the price was so good. Once again my wife demonstrated wisdom and said, "Honey, long after we have forgotten the price, we'll remember we don't really like it." We didn't buy it and have never regretted our decision. That was wisdom.

Instead of erecting more buildings, churches are learning to use the one they already have twice on Sunday morning or even three times. That's wisdom.

Our old downtown church was twelve stories high, packed out and growing. We owned only one-quarter of a block and our people parked courtesy of several downtown parking garages. Some day other garage Pharaohs might rise up who "knew not" our church and no longer allow us to use their parking garages. We couldn't ensure our own future. "Pastor," the people said, "let's buy land and relocate." That's wisdom. We did, and we're glad.

Jake Self was my associate pastor at First Southern Baptist Church in Del City, Oklahoma. He was thirty-eight when he was converted and called to the ministry. A graduate of the eighth grade, Jake said, "I may not be educated, but I can be wise." Over the decades of his life, he meticulously studied and prayed over every word in the book of Proverbs hundreds of times. Jake Self is the wisest man I have ever known. Until the last day of my pastorate, I regularly called him for advice.

If you want God to grant you wisdom, do the following:

- Read the book of Proverbs. It promises wisdom to those who read and practice its teachings.
- Ask God to reveal perspectives you've never seen.
- Get good counsel.
- Slow down.

- Pray often.
- Live close to Him.
- Ask for wisdom.
- Act in faith.

Wisdom is your heritage. Wisdom is your treasure. Wisdom is your necessity.

---

*God has united you with Christ Jesus. For our benefit God
made him to be wisdom itself. Christ made us right with God;
he made us pure and holy, and he freed us from sin.*

1 CORINTHIANS 1:30 (NLT)

*And Jesus increased in wisdom and stature,
and in favour with God and man.*

LUKE 2:52

CHAPTER 11

PRACTICE RESPECT

Privates saluting a sergeant may have no regard for the sergeant as a person, but they'd better respect the stripes on their superior's arm. Similarly, the apostle Paul neither respected the person nor the theology of the high priest. But he did respect the office.

> Paul looked straight at the Sanhedrin and said, "My brothers, I have fulfilled my duty to God in all good conscience to this day." At this the high priest Ananias ordered those standing near Paul to strike him on the mouth. Then Paul said to him, "God will strike you, you white-washed wall! You sit there to judge me according to the law, yet you yourself violate the law by commanding that I be struck!"
>
> Those who were standing near Paul said, "You dare to insult God's high priest?"
>
> Paul replied, "Brothers, I did not realize that he was the high priest; for it is written: 'Do not speak evil about the ruler of your people.'" (Acts 23:1-5, NIV)

God is a God of order, and order means rank and authority. God has placed within society a structure through which He directs the affairs of men. The persons currently holding the positions of author-ity and responsibility, whether in a church or government, business or school, may be less than perfect and their decisions flawed, but the system is still God's instrument in our lives, and the positions require our respect.

> *Obey them that have the rule over you, and submit yourselves: for they watch for your souls, as they that must give account, that they may do it with joy, and not with grief: for that is unprofitable for you.* (Hebrews 13:17)

> *Everyone must submit to governing authorities. For all authority comes from God, and those in positions of authority have been placed there by God. So anyone who rebels against authority is rebelling against what God has instituted, and they will be punished. For the authorities do not strike fear in people who are doing right, but in those who are doing wrong. Would you like to live without fear of the authorities? Do what is right, and they will honor you. The authorities are God's servants, sent for your good. But if you are doing wrong, of course you should be afraid, for they have the power to punish you. They are God's servants, sent for the very purpose of punishing those who do what is wrong. So you must submit to them, not only to avoid punishment, but also to keep a clear conscience.* (Romans 13:1-5, NLT)

God's system is flawless, but people are less than perfect and His church is composed of well-meaning but flawed leaders and members. We are all imperfect sojourners on the road to Christ-likeness, with a very, very long journey ahead. The church is a body with people of honor and dishonor; some use their gifts well, others ignore them, still others abuse them. Some spiritual gifts are less apparent than others; some are more public and prominent. But all must function together in beauty and holiness to be the church.

People make mistakes, and the living organism that is a local church, made up of people, functions with flaws. The right servants will sometimes be placed in the wrong slots in the system, causing serious problems. Even so, the system is biblical, the order necessary. The church is still Christ's body on earth. The wrong people in positions of authority are still worthy of respect because of the positions they hold. That's why when Paul realized that Ananias—whom he had just criticized—was the high priest, he apologized for being disrespectful. He changed his attitude because of his respect for the office. Similarly, even though I disagree strongly with many of the theological positions of a reigning Catholic pope, I would treat him with courtesy and respect if we met.

Practice respect.

Give to everyone what you owe them: Pay your taxes and
government fees to those who collect them, and give
respect and honor to those who are in authority.
ROMANS 13:7 (NLT)

CHAPTER 12

BE A VISIONARY

Looking for a great personal testimony? It doesn't get any better than this: "Whereupon, O king Agrippa, I was not disobedient unto the heavenly vision" (Acts 26:19).

Paul's vision was likely a bit more spectacular than yours or mine. His experience does not mean that we have to see blinding lights and audibly hear the voice of Jesus. Our vision is God's dream in our hearts, His goal in our souls. Where God wants you to go. What He wants you to become. All that was in what Paul saw in the blinding light. Ours is what we will see in our hearts.

Do you really know where you are going? Do you struggle with what you are, or celebrate what you can become?

In 1969, our pastor-*less* church called for a vote to disband. Many men had been interviewed for consideration as the new pastor. With a Sunday morning attendance of three hundred to four hundred in a 2,300-seat auditorium, other potential pastors asked, "Can we close the balcony?" I asked, "Can it be enlarged?"

Houston—the space capital, the oil capital, the medical capital, the financial capital. By my own logic I saw what it was. By God's vision I saw what it could become.

Archimedes said, "Give me a place to stand and I can move the world." Robert F. Kennedy said, "Some men see things as they are and ask, 'Why?' I dream things that never were and ask, 'Why not?'"

The essential ingredient in any opportunity is potential. The issue is never what *is*, but what it can *become*. And I think that's the way God sees us.

Two shoe salesmen went to Africa and ordered three thousand pairs of shoes. After a week one sent home a text message: "Cancel my order, these people don't wear shoes." The other: "Triple my order. Everybody in Africa needs shoes."

Make no little plans, but never forget that God's plan, even though different, is a better plan.

Seek His heart and get His vision. It's greater than anything you thought up yourself.

What circumstances has God placed in front of you that are ripe with kingdom potential? What is God's vision for you?

God gave the wise men a vision to follow the star, and they did.

God gave Thomas Edison a vision to invent a new light source, and 1,120 failures later, he did.

God gave William Carey a vision to open India to the gospel, and he did.

God gave Dawson Trotman a vision to disciple the worldwide body of Christ, and he did.

God gave Martin Luther King Jr. a vision to integrate the South, and he did.

God gave Bill Bright a vision to put trained witnesses on every college campus in America, and he did.

God gave Paul Crouch a vision to televise the gospel to the whole world, and he did.

Ask God to show you His unique vision for you. The key to finding His vision is total willingness to know and do it. The Pharisees refused to acknowledge that Jesus was the Son of God. Jesus said, "If any man will do his will, he shall know of the doctrine, whether it be of God, or whether I speak of myself" (John 7:17). The Pharisees were not willing to know the truth about Jesus. If He was who He claimed to be, they would have had to acknowledge Him as Lord and they had no intention of doing so. Jesus was saying, "Since you're not willing to know, you won't know." If that is your predicament, pray this: "Lord, I'm honestly not willing, but I am willing to be made willing."

And when He answers, don't try to evaluate the size or significance of the task. If God's vision for you is that you be a doorkeeper in His house, remember it is an important part of His greater vision for the kingdom. If someone doesn't open the door to the church, no one can come in, hear the Word, be changed, and perhaps go out and change the world. Peter opened the door of the gospel to the whole world when he preached to the Jews at Pentecost in Acts 2 and the Gentiles in Acts 10.

No vision from God is insignificant. The important thing is not the size of the vision but the Source. Nothing we do in His name and in His will is ever insignificant.

If people can't see what God is doing, they stumble all over themselves;
but when they attend to what he reveals, they are most blessed.

PROVERBS 29:18 (MSG)

CHAPTER 13

ACT JUSTLY

Recently the world was abuzz with the story of an American father whose beloved son lived with his mother and new stepfather in Brazil.

After the mother died, the father sought to get his son back. The stepfather and his family were powerful and influential people in Brazil and wanted to keep the boy. After repeated attempts, it was clear under Brazilian law they *could* keep the boy. But was it right? The answer was obvious: He belonged with his father. The world held its breath as the matter went before the chief justice of the Supreme Court of Brazil. Legally, he could have ruled that the boy stay. But the judge did the right thing and returned the boy to his father. The judge acted justly.

The simplest definition of the word *just* is "fair." The pragmatic application of the definition is "show no partiality; treat everyone alike." God calls all believers to live this way. James 2:1-4 says,

> *My dear friends, don't let public opinion influence how you live out our glorious, Christ-originated faith. If a man enters your church wearing an expensive suit, and a street person wearing rags comes in right after him, and you say to the man in the suit, "Sit here, sir; this is the best seat in the house!" and either ignore the street person or say, "Better sit here in the back row," haven't you segregated God's children and proved that you are judges who can't be trusted?* (MSG)

Acting justly means not showing partiality to anyone. Why? Because the basis of all partiality is self-serving. I give deference to the attractive, the influential, and the wealthy. My motive: to receive something from them—attention, promotion, compliments, position, possessions. It's all about me. I show favoritism toward you for my benefit, not yours.

But it's not about me. We should have learned that a long time ago. A very, very long time ago—at Calvary.

People can see through partiality like the empty suit it is: pure selfishness, unadulterated self-centeredness.

We treat people fairly by giving our full attention to the person in front of us rather than looking past him or her to see if there is someone more attractive, better dressed, or more important we'd rather talk with.

Treat everyone alike.

Be fair.

Be impartial.

Do the right thing.

When your life is over and people walk away from your grave, would you rather they say, "She was so talented!" "He was the most successful businessman I know," or "_____ (insert your name here) was a good person, a really good person"?

Remember, God doesn't just suggest we treat people justly and fairly; He requires it. Listen to His declaration to Israel.

> *And what does the LORD require of you?*
> *To act justly and to love mercy*
> *   and to walk humbly with your God.* (Micah 6:8, NIV, emphasis added)

I think this may be the best summation of a good man or woman found anywhere in Scripture:

Act justly.

Love mercy.

Walk humbly.

As darkness requires light to see, as lungs require air to breathe, so God requires you to be a *good person* if you are to be *His person.* The road to goodness, fairness, and impartiality runs through mercy and humility. We'll explore these two characteristics in the next two chapters.

A lover of hospitality, a lover of good men, sober, just, holy, temperate.

TITUS 1:8

CHAPTER 14

LOVE MERCY

The story is told of a politician who, after receiving the proofs of a portrait, was angry with the photographer. He stormed into his office and said, "This picture does not do me justice!" The photographer replied, "Sir, with a face like yours, you don't need justice, you need mercy."

God's mercy is not only a far more serious issue, it is our greatest need. I've often wondered why someone didn't write a song called "Amazing Mercy." It could have easily become the most beloved hymn in the world.

Luke 6:36 says, "Therefore be merciful, just as your Father also is merciful" (NKJV).

Mercy is one thing I get. It is my spiritual gift. It has never crossed my mind to kick a man when he's down, to rub it in, to give him what he deserves, to expose him. I will carry things to the grave that I know about people. I always tend toward no penalty at all. Let others off the hook. Go easy. Let it go. Forgive and forget. Forgive and walk away.

And you know what? I've experienced the truth of Matthew 5:7: "Blessed are the merciful: for they shall obtain mercy." My life has been characterized by people being easy on me—the policeman on the corner, the judge in traffic court, the teacher in the classroom, my mom at home (unlike my dad, who beat the thunder out of me when I deserved it, which was often!).

Let's be clear in our definition of terms. *Grace* means "getting what you don't deserve." Forgiveness, blessing, peace—all the good stuff. *Mercy*, on the other hand, means "not getting what you *do* deserve." Exposure, judgment, penalty—all the bad stuff.

Micah 6:8 tells us that God requires us to "love mercy." Not just tolerate or even practice it, but truly, passionately love it. People come to God through His mercy, and we must show mercy to others—even when we are tempted to get back at those who have been unjust to us.

Joseph was a powerful example of what it means to love mercy. His brothers sold him into slavery when he was just a teenager. Years later, when he came to power in Egypt, the tables were turned. Now their lives were in *his* hands. It was *his* chance to get even. But when the time came, Joseph forgave, welcomed, and embraced his brothers—and wept bitterly. Joseph is the most complete picture of Jesus in the Old Testament, and he should be a picture of each of us.

We all make bad decisions; everyone fails at one time or another. But God's people are to be a forgiving people. Every time we forgive a coworker, friend, relative, or neighbor, we should do so fully conscious of our own failures. Mercy puts us in the other person's shoes. Mercy practices the Golden Rule.

It's important that mercy be paired up with wisdom, so ask God to help you understand when to show mercy. I've found that people with the gift of mercy can lack discernment, which is why wisdom is critical. What kind of society would we have if no one ever paid for any wrong done, any crime committed? Wisdom discerns when the depth of repentance and commitment to change is genuine to the point of receiving mercy. And that can be difficult to discern for someone who really likes people.

Let's face it. God requires us to be good, and Micah 6:8 clearly spells out the *how*: "To act justly and to love mercy and to walk humbly with your God" (NIV). What a powerful prescription for becoming a good person. Someone like Joseph, someone like Jesus.

But the wisdom from above is first of all pure. It is also peace loving,
gentle at all times, and willing to yield to others. It is full of mercy
and good deeds. It shows no favoritism and is always sincere.

JAMES 3:17 (NLT)

CHAPTER 15

WALK HUMBLY

Justice, mercy, and humility are a trinity, each a reflection of the other. "He that is greatest among you shall be your servant" (Matthew 23:11).

Some people have little choice in the matter of humility. They have not *humbled themselves* under the mighty hand of God as much as they have *been humbled* by their status in life. Humility is far better when it's chosen.

You have two choices: Humble yourself and be exalted or exalt yourself and be humbled. The two potentially greatest evangelists I ever heard were the most arrogant, unteachable people I have ever known. Today, they conduct no crusades at all.

I recently attempted to shake hands with one of today's brightest young leaders. After I introduced myself, he replied, "I know who you are," and walked away.

King Saul was tall, handsome, charismatic, and on top of the world. But he was proud and self-centered. David was a gentle, humble shepherd boy. God rejected Saul from being king: "I have found David the son of Jesse, a man after mine own heart" (Acts 13:22).

The heart of Jesus is a heart of humility.

Think of yourselves the way Christ Jesus thought of himself. He had equal status with God but didn't think so much of himself that he had to cling to the advantages of that status no matter what. Not at all. When the time came, he set aside the privileges of deity and took on the status of a slave, became human! Having become human, he stayed human. It was an incredibly humbling process. He didn't claim special privileges. Instead, he lived a selfless, obedient life and then died a selfless, obedient death—and the worst kind of death at that—a crucifixion.

Because of that obedience, God lifted him high and honored him far beyond anyone or anything, ever, so that all created beings in heaven and on earth—even those long ago dead and buried—will bow in worship before this Jesus Christ, and call out in praise that he is the Master of all, to the glorious honor of God the Father. (Philippians 2:5-11, MSG)

Humility never takes the credit, seeks the spotlight, or wants the glory. Humility means "I never forget where I came from," which is nowhere at all. Humility knows what I can do apart from Him, which is nothing at all.

Jesus never did anything without the Father, and He tells us, "Without Me you can do nothing" (John 15:5, NKJV). *Nothing*. It's a compound word. *No thing—a thing that does not exist.* That's who I am and what I can do without Him. Jesus didn't say "not much." He said "*nothing.*"

I can't talk about humility without being reminded of Billy Graham. Billy's the kid who used to live next door. You know, the guy who went to your high school, the guy who dated your sister. I twice had a private conversation with him, about an hour as I recall. I couldn't get him to talk about himself. He only wanted to talk about me. And I thought, *Now I know the secret of Billy Graham.*

Humility turns the conversation to talk about you, not about me. Humility handles success with grace and class. Humility starts at the foot of the cross—and stays there.

Jesus—crown of heaven, adored by angels, darling of the Trinity—laid aside His regal robes of royalty, stepped to earth through the womb of the virgin, made Himself of no reputation, became sin for us, and died in our place. As we follow in His steps, we would do well to lay aside our regal robes as well.

*He hath shown thee, O man, what is good; and what
doth the LORD require of thee, but to do justly, and to
love mercy, and to walk humbly with thy God?*
MICAH 6:8

CHAPTER 16

HAVE FAITH

By faith Noah built an ark. By faith Abraham left his home. By faith Sarah conceived a son. By faith Joseph, when he was about to die, said that the Israelites would leave Egypt and asked them to take his bones with them when they did. "Faith is the confidence that what we hope for will actually happen; it gives us assurance about things we cannot see. Through their faith, the people in days of old earned a good reputation" (Hebrews 11:1-2, NLT).

By faith the children of Israel came out of bondage in Egypt and through the wilderness to the border of the Promised Land. It was time to go forward. God is never pleased when His children are content to simply stand still. Joshua and Caleb had faith that they could successfully conquer the land. The other ten spies said, "No way! Too many giants, great armies, fortified cities."

The Old Testament saints paid a great price for their faith in the promised Messiah. Though they never lived to see Him, He came.

Others experienced mockings and scourgings, yes, also chains and imprisonment. They were stoned, they were sawn in two, they were tempted, they were put to death with the sword; they went about in sheepskins, in goatskins, being destitute, afflicted, ill-treated (men of whom the world was not worthy), wandering in deserts and mountains and caves and holes in the ground.

*And all these, having gained approval through their faith, did
not receive what was promised, because God had provided something
better for us, so that apart from us they would not be made perfect.*
(Hebrews 11:36-40, NASB)

Never forget, there's always a reason not to go forward. From the
days of the Roman Empire, there *have been* and always *will be* obstacles,
opposition, problems, and excuses. Real-life giants abound. But the decision to go forward is always made in faith. The work of the kingdom
always advances on the wings of faith. Only the few who believed entered
the Promised Land and lived. The doubters returned to the wilderness
and died. "These things happened to them as examples for us. They were
written down to warn us who live at the end of the age" (1 Corinthians
10:11, NLT).

Need we remind ourselves it's called the Christian *faith?* Everything
God has done in the past is intended to encourage our faith that He can
and will do it again. "And the LORD said to Moses, 'How long will these
people treat me with contempt? Will they never believe me, even after all
the miraculous signs I have done among them?'" (Numbers 14:11, NLT).
God did not ask, "Why don't they understand Me? Why can't they calcu-
late what I'm doing? Why don't they figure Me out?" His question was
"Why don't they *believe* Me?"

The church of Jesus Christ has always made her greatest advance in
times of greatest difficulty by faith. Under the penalty of death, first-
century believers declared allegiance not to Nero, but to Jesus. And the
church grew exponentially.

Since the late 1940s, the body of Christ has prayed diligently for the
church in China, struggling to survive under Communist rule. Most
estimates place today's Christian population in China beyond one
hundred million believers. In spite of overwhelming odds, the church in
China continues to flourish in faith.

The difference in going forward *in faith* and not going forward *by
sight* is enormous.

Our calling is never a call to sight, but to faith.

Bushes can't burn and not be consumed.

Red Seas don't part, leaving a dry path people can walk on.

Lame men don't walk.

Saviors don't rise from the dead.

Or do they?

There are only two roads in the world of service and ministry: sight and faith. "The just shall live by faith" (Romans 1:17).

In both my churches, we never *saw* how we could reasonably do anything we ever did. Every great advance was accomplished by *faith*. In 1972, Houston's First Baptist voted to relocate and build new buildings. The contractor told us the price would be $3.2 million. The lowest bid was $8.1 million. We had to make a choice: remain small and accomplish little, or step out in faith and accomplish much. We chose the latter, by faith!

Every great decision is made with an element of risk. And that's where faith comes in. The confirmation always comes after the commitment. The lights don't come on until you turn the switch.

God blesses those who trust Him. Since Abraham left Ur, God has never failed a person who stepped out on His promises in faith. *And you won't be the first.*

"Faith cometh by hearing, and hearing by the word of God" (Romans 10:17).

Read it. Stand on it. And don't make other provisions, just in case. Faith brings victory, and each victory builds more faith for the next.

Every great work for God began as a dream in the heart and became reality by faith. God is faithful! Have faith. And remember: Faith is not believing God *can*; faith is believing God *will*!

---

*And it is impossible to please God without faith. Anyone
who wants to come to him must believe that God exists
and that he rewards those who sincerely seek him.*

HEBREWS 11:6 (NLT)

CHAPTER 17

BUILD THE KINGDOM

Self-centered people seldom make it all the way to the finish line. The kingdom-minded person will finish the journey much more often than the *my* kingdom–minded person.

Today there is too much emphasis on *my* class, *my* church, *my* ministry. Sadly, I don't see the passion for God's greater kingdom in some of today's young leaders that I saw in their fathers.

Perhaps it's plain old selfishness and pride. Or simply the high-powered promotion of our culture. The old "Me Generation" mentality: You owe it to yourself. Go ahead, you deserve it. But we don't deserve first place. He does. His kingdom does. He made it clear in Matthew 6:33 when He said, "Seek the Kingdom of God above all else, and live righteously, and he will give you everything you need" (NLT).

My heart was deeply stirred when our Houston Association of Churches pointed out sixty-seven dying inner-city congregations that would close and disband within a year without help. We began pouring money, time, and people into them.

I asked our people to go serve in them, and many did. Every Sunday I gave two invitations: *join* the church or *leave* the church to serve elsewhere. Sixty-two of the sixty-seven survived and thrive today. We built a culture of missions in our church, and more than eight hundred of our members heard God's call, went to seminary, were ordained, and entered full-time Christian ministry—and are still in it.

Today on any given Sunday, there are twice as many in all those churches and the missions they planted combined as in the mother church. We didn't grow much during that time, but His kingdom grew exponentially. And we are grateful.

Every course you pursue, every decision you make, must be set against the backdrop of this question: "Does it expand God's kingdom—or mine?"

Be a kingdom woman.

Be a kingdom man.

Build the kingdom—*His kingdom*!

P. N. Kurien is the legendary leader of the All India Prayer Fellowship. It is a massive ministry touching uncounted lives for the Master. When he discovered he had Parkinson's disease and was no longer able to continue his ministry, his son Koshy Kurien, a renowned orthopedic surgeon in New Delhi, left his prosperous practice to continue the further expansion of his father's ministry.

Today, the ministry consists of the All India Prayer Fellowship Hospital, a grade school, and the India Bible Institute & Immanuel Theological Seminary, which trains and sends out thousands of evangelists across the continent. Koshy Kurien left *his* kingdom for *God's* kingdom. We must do no less.

For Yours is the kingdom and the power and the glory forever. Amen.
MATTHEW 6:13 (NKJV)

CHAPTER 18

STAY COMMITTED

The crowd at Passover was overwhelming. The village of Jerusalem often swelled to overflowing during Passover week.

The people were anxious to see the young upstart prophet from Nazareth, who claimed to be the Messiah and was healing the blind and raising the dead.

When He did so before their very eyes, the response was overwhelming.

> *Now when he was in Jerusalem at the passover, in the feast day, many believed in his name, when they saw the miracles which he did. But Jesus did not commit himself unto them, because he knew all men, and needed not that any should testify of man: for he knew what was in man.* (John 2:23-25)

John doesn't even attempt to number the crowd. He simply uses the generic term *many*. You can be certain the number was very large. And what does the Master do? Send the disciples out among them with decision cards and gospels of John? No. He doesn't even acknowledge their response, but turns and walks away.

The reason is buried in verse 24: "He knew all men." Jesus looked in their hearts and saw they only responded because of the miracles. They were more excited about *what He had done* than *who He was*. He knew that when the miracles were gone, they'd be gone. He did not commit Himself to them because they had not committed themselves to Him.

The nature of Christian commitment is 100 percent, and it's irrevocable. Commitment is by definition not temporary. Commitment means once and for all. Commitment means it's for real. Commitment means it's for life. It's a marriage to Jesus Christ, and once it takes place, it never ends.

Suppose I were to ask you, "Is your husband faithful to you? Is your wife faithful to you?" How many of you would respond, "Well, yes, he's pretty faithful." Or "She's a pretty faithful woman." Do you really want to be married to someone who's just "pretty faithful"?

There are no degrees of faithfulness. You are either faithful or you're not.

Jesus made it clear when He said, "You are truly my disciples if you remain faithful to my teachings" (John 8:31, NLT).

Continuing faithfully does not *make* you His disciple. It validates the fact that you *are* His disciple. Continuation, commitment, and endless discipleship authenticate your profession of faith.

Paul said, "By grace are ye saved through faith" (Ephesians 2:8). James said, "Faith without works is dead" (James 2:26). Paul and James were not two combatants on opposite sides of the issue; they were soldiers standing back-to-back, fending off two different false doctrines. Paul addressed the false doctrine that you can be saved by works, and James that you can be saved by talk.

Making a pseudo profession of faith, without enduring commitment, means nothing. If your faith means *anything*, it means *everything*. If it's real, it will last. Call it what you want: "Becoming a Christian," "being saved," "getting converted," "being born again," "accepting Christ" — it comes down to the same thing. The nature of salvation is an *unending commitment to Jesus Christ.*

You don't hold out; He holds you. But if He's really holding you, your life will show it. If your commitment doesn't last, it's not because you lost your salvation. It's likely you never had it in the first place.

"Saving faith" endures. That is its nature. I can't count the times I heard Adrian Rogers say, "The faith that fizzles before the finish was flawed from the first."

The same thing is true of your call to follow Jesus. Don't even think about quitting. The gifts and calling of God are irrevocable: "For the gifts and calling of God are without repentance" (Romans 11:29).

You don't wake up every morning and recommit to follow Him. "Wherever He leads I'll go, whatever He says I'll do" has no escape clause.

Commitment means commitment. Faithful means faithful. Don't be AWOL. Don't fail the One who called you. Your Lord loves you. Your family and friends trust you. Your church community believes in you. Your world needs you.

Stay committed.

Don't be afraid of what you are about to suffer. The devil will throw some of you into prison to test you. You will suffer for ten days. But if you remain faithful even when facing death, I will give you the crown of life.
REVELATION 2:10 (NLT)

CHAPTER 19

SETTLE THE CALL

God calls us to do what He wants us to do. Many Christians assume God calls only some to full-time ministry. Not so. All Christians are in full-time ministry.

You can't make the journey unless you know you're on the bus. You can't make the flight until you get on the plane. Let's go back to square one and nail down precisely what He's called you to do in your own unique way.

And may I say, it's not the end of the world if you read this chapter and say, "I'm out of God's will." More than one person has been honest enough, man enough, woman enough, to say, "I missed it. I'm in the wrong job, wrong profession, wrong ministry, wrong place."

There's nothing wrong with that; in fact, there's something honest and even heroic about it. There *is* something wrong with continuing to act the part when you haven't been called to fill the role.

From salesman to secretary, from lawyer to landlord, from doctor to developer, here are five tests to know what God has called you to do.

1. Desire. Psalm 37:4 says, "Delight yourself also in the LORD, and He shall give you the desires of your heart" (NKJV). God promises to give you the desire of your heart if He is your delight and passion. Your desires and His will shall be the same. The promise is at once natural and simple. If you love Him with all your heart, you will love what He loves. His will for you *will* become your will, and you *will* want to do it more than anything in the world. The question is not "Shall I enter this profession or that?" The question is "Do I love Him with all my heart?" If the answer is yes, then do what you want to do, because you'll want to do the *right thing*. For me, the right thing is pastoring and preaching. For you, the right thing might be practicing medicine or being a stay-at-home mom.

2. Ability. What do you do? What do you like? Who are you? What are your gifts? What comes naturally? God doesn't call the blind to be truck drivers or the tone deaf to be musicians. What He wants you to do, He has gifted and capacitated you to do.

3. Opportunity. God will open the doors for you to do what He wants you to do. Try every door. If they're closed, consider something else. What He calls you to do, He will make possible for you to do.

4. Blessing. When you do what you think you are called to do, there will be some degree of God's affirmation upon your work.

5. Counsel. The opinion of others matters. Talk to the spiritually mature who know you well. There is much wisdom in many counselors. "For by wise counsel you will wage your own war, and in a multitude of counselors there is safety" (Proverbs 24:6, NKJV).

When I was considering moving from Del City to Houston, the Lord impressed upon me to call a wise friend for counsel. Dr. W. T. Furr, pastor of the great Queensborough Baptist Church in Shreveport, said, "John, I've learned an important truth about God's direction in a move. They may happen in either order, but there will come a *release* from the old and a *passion* for the new." Both happened. Dr. Furr was right. I moved. Seek good counsel.

These five tests form a cluster of truth. Take your time, be faithful, test the waters, and pray it through. If there is still uncertainty, wait. He will make it clear—in His time.

*While they were ministering to the Lord
and fasting, the Holy Spirit said,
"Set apart for Me Barnabas and Saul for the
work to which I have called them."*

ACTS 13:2 (NASB)

CHAPTER 20

LOVE UNCONDITIONALLY

King David paid severely for his sin. "Fourfold," he said to the prophet Nathan, and fourfold it was.

- King David had his heart set on Bathsheba's baby. After just seven days, the baby died (see 2 Samuel 12:18).
- David's son Amnon raped his sister Tamar (see 2 Samuel 13:8-14).
- Absalom, David's son, murdered Amnon (see 2 Samuel 13:20-33).
- Absalom attempted to dethrone David, his own father (see 2 Samuel 15:1-14).

David's response to the news of Absalom's rebellion and death gives great insight into what made him *a man after God's own heart*.

Though Absalom tried to kill David and take his throne, David loved his son unconditionally. When the courier brought the message, "Good news, David, the rebellion is put down, the kingdom secure, and *Absalom is dead*," what was David's response? "I'm glad you are dead, you rascal. You deserved it. Thank God, my kingdom is secure! It's great that I'm still on the throne"? Not at all!

Listen to David's heart. "And the king was much moved, and went up to the chamber over the gate, and wept: and as he went, thus he said, O my son Absalom, my son, my son Absalom! *would God I had died for thee*, O Absalom, my son, my son!" (2 Samuel 18:33, emphasis added).

> David, Israel's great king
>> Solomon's great example
>>> Jesus' honored ancestor

No wonder God called David a man after His own heart (see Acts 13:22). David's loving response was the opposite of a father with whom I came in contact during a great youth revival we were having at First Baptist in 1972. We called it SPIRENO, an acrostic for "Spiritual Revolution Now." Eleven thousand teenagers made decisions for Christ, more than four thousand for the first time. SPIRENO was written up in *Reader's Digest, Time,* and *Newsweek.* SPIRENO captured the attention of America.

A television executive on the East Coast read about SPIRENO and asked us to find his son, a runaway in the underground drug culture of Houston. We found the boy and led him to Christ, and then he wanted to go home.

I called his dad with the good news as the boy listened to the conversation.

Sadly, his dad's response was, "How long is his hair? Will he apologize to his mom? Is he willing to go back to college?" The boy, listening in, dropped the phone and ran out to the street, and I never heard from him again — nor, to my knowledge, has his dad.

The dad loved the boy, but not unconditionally. If the son did what the dad wanted — cut his hair like dad wanted and went to college where dad wanted — *then* he loved him.

But that is *not* unconditional love, and that is *not* the way God loves us. As surely as if I were the only sinner in the whole world, it was me He loved. It was for me He died — for my sin, all my sin.

When Peter denied Christ, I was there. When Judas betrayed Him, I was there. When Pilate condemned Him, I was there. When Rome crucified Him, I was there. I did it. I'm guilty. I've done it all. Yet He loves me without exception.

He loved me, not when I was whole, but when I was broken.

Not clean, but unclean.

Not pure, but defiled.

Not righteous, but filthy.

Not compliant, but rebellious.

Without prior condition.

Without merit.

Without reservation.

He loved me as I was, and He loved me *unconditionally.*

If I would live as He lived, I must love as He loved. People may betray you, lie about you, and be downright mean to you. But you must forgive them. You must treat them with grace. You must overlook their faults. Real love has no prior conditions, no restraint, and no limits. We love because God lives in our hearts through Christ, and it is His nature to love *unconditionally.*

But God demonstrates His own love toward us,
in that while we were still sinners, Christ died for us.
ROMANS 5:8 (NKJV)

CHAPTER 21

BE AN OVERCOMER

Let's cut to the chase. Satan does not want you to finish strong. He's out to decimate your life and destroy your service to the Master. But we've got his number. "Keep a cool head. Stay alert. The Devil is poised to pounce, and would like nothing better than to catch you napping. Keep your guard up" (1 Peter 5:8, MSG).

- Pastors will tell you that only one-third of their members attend church on any given Sunday.
- Only five in one hundred believers have ever led a soul to Christ.
- In his book *Revolution*, George Barna reports that one-third of churched Christians say they tithe while fewer than 10 percent actually do.[3]
- For nearly six decades I have personally documented that only one or two of every ten friends in ministry continue to serve until age sixty-five.
- In his book *Pastors at Greater Risk*, H. B. London said, "57 percent of pastors say they would leave the pastorate if they could do some other vocation and 1,500 pastors leave the ministry each month."[4]

We can do better.

The simple truth, the powerful truth, is this: You only have one hope, one answer, one way to victory: the Word of God.

Here are fifteen truths you've got to know and fifteen scriptures you can rely on:

1. *Expect the attack.* It's coming and it will be relentless. "Stay alert! Watch out for your great enemy, the devil. He prowls around like a roaring lion, looking for someone to devour" (1 Peter 5:8, NLT).

2. *Appropriate a victory already won.* "I have told you these things, so that in me you may have peace. In this world you will have trouble. But take heart! I have overcome the world" (John 16:33, NIV). Jesus didn't say He *will* overcome the world. He said I *have already* overcome it. We go into battle from a position of victory. Ours is not to win the battle, but to stand by faith in the power of the One who has *already* won it.

3. *Satan has nothing new.* Grade him A in persistence and consistency. Grade him F in creativity and originality. "Lest Satan should get an advantage of us: for we are not ignorant of his devices" (2 Corinthians 2:11).

4. *Sin always begins the same way.* Go back to the garden. Nothing's changed:

- The lust of the eyes — "and when the woman saw" (Genesis 3:6)
- The lust of the flesh — "and he did eat" (verse 6)
- The pride of life — "ye shall be as gods" (verse 5)

"For all that is in the world, the lust of the flesh, and the lust of the eyes, and the pride of life, is not of the Father, but is of the world" (1 John 2:16).

5. *Rely on the Word.* "And take the helmet of salvation, and the sword of the Spirit, which is the word of God" (Ephesians 6:17).

Only the Holy Spirit can defeat the Evil One. When we quote Scripture, we place a powerful sword in the hands of the Holy Spirit with which to fight our battle and win our victory.

Then Jesus was led by the Spirit into the wilderness to be tempted there by the devil. For forty days and forty nights he fasted and became very hungry.

During that time the devil came and said to him, "If you are the Son of God, tell these stones to become loaves of bread."

But Jesus told him, "No! The Scriptures say,

'People do not live by bread alone,
but by every word that comes from the mouth of God.'"

Then the devil took him to the holy city, Jerusalem, to the highest point of the Temple, and said, "If you are the Son of God, jump off! For the Scriptures say,

'He will order his angels to protect you.
And they will hold you up with their hands
so you won't even hurt your foot on a stone.'"

Jesus responded, "The Scriptures also say, 'You must not test the LORD your God.'"

Next the devil took him to the peak of a very high mountain and showed him all the kingdoms of the world and their glory. "I will give it all to you," he said, "if you will kneel down and worship me."

"Get out of here, Satan," Jesus told him. "For the Scriptures say,

'You must worship the LORD your God
and serve only him.'"

Then the devil went away, and angels came and took care of Jesus. (Matthew 4:1-11, NLT)

Three temptations offered.
Three scriptures quoted.
Three victories won.
Final score: Jesus: 3; Satan: zip.

6. *Take action.* Be smart. Jesus called it being "wise as serpents, and harmless as doves" (Matthew 10:16).

- Never be alone with a member of the opposite sex.
- Put a window in your office door.
- Avoid the second look. Job said, "I have made a covenant with my eyes; why then should I look upon a young woman?" (Job 31:1, NKJV). There are looks and then there are looks. It's the second look that leads to second thoughts, and they lead to trouble. Get on the offensive. Swing into action. You're in a battle for your life.

7. *Be accountable.* Covenant Eyes and X3 Watch are excellent programs for your computer—for both men and women. Potiphar's wife could have used such a program. Choose one and start an accountability group. Help each other.

> *Likewise you younger people, submit yourselves to your elders. Yes, all of you be submissive to one another, and be clothed with humility, for*
>> *"God resists the proud,*
>> *But gives grace to the humble."* (1 Peter 5:5, NKJV)

8. *Be encouraged.* Time spent fighting God's battles is not time wasted. Each victory makes us stronger. "Submit yourselves therefore to God. Resist the devil, and he will flee from you" (James 4:7).

9. *Sin always has a surprise ending.* Drop the pebble in the pond and you have no idea where the ripples will end. "So they hanged Haman on the gallows that he had prepared for Mordecai" (Esther 7:10).

10. *The marks of sin remain indelibly.* The *guilt* of sin is immediately removed upon confession and repentance. The *consequences* of sin are quite a different story. Murder a man and God will forgive you. But the man will still be dead. "From this time on, your family will live by the sword because you have despised me by taking Uriah's wife to be your own" (2 Samuel 12:10, NLT).

11. *The effect of sin is passed on to others.* "You must not bow down to them or worship them, for I, the LORD your God, am a jealous God who will not tolerate your affection for any other gods. I lay the sins of the parents upon their children; the entire family is affected—even children in the third and fourth generations of those who reject me" (Exodus 20:5, NLT). My children and their children do not *pay* for my sin, but they are *impacted* by my sin.

12. *You can't beat the odds in the game of sin.* As we tremble before sin's allure, Satan whispers, "You're different." "You're the exception." "You won't get caught." "No one will ever know." But God allows no exceptions, strikes no bargains, has no pets, plays no favorites, and makes no deals. *And He won't start with you.* "If you fail to keep your word, then you will have sinned against the LORD, and you may be sure that your sin will find you out" (Numbers 32:23, NLT).

13. *The greatest thrill of sin is always the first time.* Each successive sin requires more and more of the same to equal the thrill of the first. *And that is the nature of addiction.* "Temptation comes from our own desires, which entice us and drag us away. These desires give birth to sinful actions. And when sin is allowed to grow, it gives birth to death" (James 1:14-15, NLT).

14. *You can win the battle against temptation.* See 1 Corinthians 10:13 and Revelation 12:11. Satan gave it his best shot, and Jesus quoted God's Word. "Then the devil left him, and angels came and attended him" (Matthew 4:11, NIV).

15. *Forgiven sin is forgotten sin.* "As far as the east is from the west, so far hath he removed our transgressions from us" (Psalm 103:12). "And their sins and iniquities will I remember no more" (Hebrews 10:17).

If you want to finish well, read the Bible. Read it often. Read it consistently. Read it early. Pray it. Love it and live it. It's your only hope for being an overcomer.

---

*They overcame him by the blood of the Lamb
and by the word of their testimony; they did not
love their lives so much as to shrink from death.*

Revelation 12:11 (NIV)

CHAPTER 22

BE YOURSELF

I n Matthew 22, Jesus commanded,

> *"You shall love the Lord your God with all your heart, and
> with all your soul, and with all your mind." This is the great and
> foremost commandment. The second is like it, "You shall love your
> neighbor as yourself." On these two commandments depend the
> whole Law and the Prophets.* (verses 37-40, NASB)

Loving yourself is normal. Loving yourself is healthy. Loving yourself is not pride, ego, or narcissism. In Christ, it's a secure self-image, not
just of *who* I am but of *whose* and *what* I am *in Him.* Insecure people are
weak people. Insecure people don't know who they are because they
don't know who they are *in Christ.* Secure people do.

"You shall love the Lord your God with all your heart, and
with all your soul, and with all your strength, and with all
your mind; and your neighbor as yourself" (Luke 10:27, NASB).

It's *wonderful* to love God

It's *commanded* to love others.

It's *normal* to love yourself.

Because I'm okay *in Him,* I can say, "You're okay." Perhaps you're
thinking, *Me? Okay?* That's right: not somebody else, *YOU.* You really
are okay, you know. Don't try to be somebody else. Don't get all stressed

out and uptight trying to be who you're not. Be you. Be *who* you are, *why* you are, and *what* you are. That's essential to your witness. Be yourself.

The *likeability factor* is huge. When people like you, they're comfortable around you. If they can't relate to you, the odds that they will be open to your witness and your influence go way down. Quickly. And relating to you doesn't happen if you're not yourself. A secure self—*in Him.* Don't let the messenger get in the way of the message.

For the first several years of my ministry, I was not sure who I really was as a preacher. In the pulpit, I was mostly the last guy I had heard. I can bring down the house at a pastor's conference with my imitations of all the preachers I *used to be.* My style was oratorical, and it was an affected style. When I discovered the more conversational style of preaching, I discovered the real me—and became more comfortable and more effective. You can't be someone else and make it as a minister, or as a layperson. Be authentic. Be yourself.

Remember, when God made you He didn't make you like Joe Jones or Jane Doe. He made *you.* He doesn't want you to become somebody else. If He had, He could have saved you and Himself a whole lot of trouble and just made somebody else.

If you're out of your naturalness, you're out of character and out of your giftedness. Lose your uniqueness and lose your maximum usefulness to the One who made you who you are. Conferred titles give glory to men. Your uniqueness gives glory to God. And never forget people can spot an actor a mile off. People can only be comfortable with *you* as *you.*

The religious establishment despised Jesus and crucified Him. Little wonder. They were a bunch of phonies. Playing the part was what being a Pharisee was all about.

The high and mighty hated Him. But the "common people heard him gladly" (Mark 12:37). The sick and simple loved Him.

Be yourself. If you're the real deal, people will believe in you and follow you as you follow Him.

Years ago God wrote these words on my heart, *"So live, that no one will ever suspect you're a preacher, but if they find out you are, they won't be surprised."*

Have you ever heard of fool's gold? It's iron pyrite, shiny and yellow just like real gold, but it is very much lighter in weight. It doesn't have the same substance as gold, and it doesn't behave the same under pressure. That's a pretty good description of inauthentic material in the hands of the Master Craftsman.

Pastor or politician, lawyer or lumberjack, homemaker or hotel manager—*just be you!*

It is God himself who has made us what we are and given us new lives from Christ Jesus; and long ages ago he planned that we should spend these lives in helping others.
EPHESIANS 2:10 (TLB)

CHAPTER 23

CULTIVATE CONFIDENCE

Jehoshaphat: unusual name, special man.

He prayed, "Lord, I've got a problem—a big one—and have no idea what to do about it. But one thing *I do have* is absolute, bulletproof, unshakable confidence in You . . . *our eyes are on You*" (see 2 Chronicles 20:12).

Forty-six times the Bible tells us to be confident—to have confidence. Merriam-Webster defines *confidence* as "bold self-assurance, a state of trust or intimacy."

I was not surprised to find those two words, *bold* and *trust*, joined together in the definition of *confidence*. To know Him is to love Him. To love Him is to trust Him. To trust Him is to be emboldened by Him.

Like a great athlete, the Christian becomes strong through exercise, the practice of our faith, and diet, the meat of His Word. Read it. Assimilate it. Live it. You'll find God's Word to be the primary vitamin—vitamin B-confident.

- Confidence in Him. "For the LORD will be your confidence" (Proverbs 3:26, NKJV).
- Confidence in His presence. "I will never leave you nor forsake you" (Hebrews 13:5, NKJV).
- Confidence in His provision. "My God shall supply all your

need according to His riches in glory by Christ Jesus"
(Philippians 4:19, NKJV).

- Confidence in His power. "I can do all things through Christ
who strengthens me" (Philippians 4:13, NKJV).

When we walk hand in hand with Jesus, His way will become our way. Confidence in what He will do in us, where He is leading us, is inseparably linked to our walk with Him. And in that is quiet, peaceful certainty. Confidence.

How transparent is the prayer of Jehoshaphat. How honest. How human. "We have no might against this great company that cometh against us; neither know we what to do: *but our eyes are upon thee*" (2 Chronicles 20:12, emphasis added).

Jehoshaphat, godly king of Judah, found himself facing an insurmountable horde of Moabites and Ammonites, who threatened Israel's very existence. Jehoshaphat humbled himself and prayed for deliverance from God. Early in the morning, he mustered his army and marched into battle singing praises to the Lord. God went ahead of him and decimated his enemy.

Like Jehoshapat, confident people don't stare at the problem; they fix their eyes on the Problem Solver. They don't measure the size of the dog in the fight; they measure the size of the fight in the dog. God's children don't measure the size of the problem. They don't have to; they already know God is bigger.

Confidence is not a shot in the dark, an "I hope so," "I think so," "maybe so," or "here goes nothing." Confidence is not cocky; it's certain. It's not self-centered; it's secure. "Our eyes are upon thee" (2 Chronicles 20:12).

Confident in Him. Confident in His Word. Confident in His will. I will not be moved. I will take the time for Him to accomplish what He promised and complete what He began. "Our eyes are upon Thee." You can't look at God and look at the problem at the same time. Turn your eyes upon Jesus.

That's what brought Nehemiah through. His tenacity is legendary. In spite of opposition and ridicule, in spite of discouragement and apparent hopelessness, he built the wall—*and finished it.* "When all our enemies heard the news and all the surrounding nations saw it, our enemies totally lost their nerve. They knew that God was behind this work" (Nehemiah 6:16, MSG).

Strong believers don't get discouraged; they get to digging. They don't give up; they give out more energy, more time, and more faith. They don't panic; they pursue. They don't look at the problem; they look at the Lord.

In the Cherokee Indian youth's rite of passage, his father takes him into the forest blindfolded and leaves him—alone. He is required to sit on a stump all night. He cannot cry out for help to anyone. He must remain in silence. Once he survives the night, he is a *man.* The boy is terrified. He hears all kinds of noises around him, but he sits stoically, never removing his blindfold. It is the only way he can become a man. Finally, after a horrifying night, the sun appears and he is permitted to remove his blindfold. It is then he sees his father, sitting on the stump next to him, at watch the entire night. No matter how dark the night, our Father is always there.

Build the wall.

The name of the LORD *is a strong fortress;*
the godly run to him and are safe.
PROVERBS 18:10 (NLT)

CHAPTER 24

FAMILY FIRST

F amily first. Remember those words. If you can't get it right at home, you will likely never get it right anywhere. Lose your marriage; lose it all.

Here's how it works: The Lord first, family second, everything else third. It's a bit of a wonder, a mystery perhaps, but it's really the way it is.

"My thoughts are nothing like your thoughts," says the LORD.
"And my ways are far beyond anything you could imagine. For just as the heavens are higher than the earth, so my ways are higher than your ways and my thoughts higher than your thoughts."
(Isaiah 55:8-9, NLT)

Seek first the kingdom of God and His righteousness, and He provides the food, clothing, and shelter. Put your physical needs first, and have no guarantee of either His provision or His kingdom.

Keep all your money and end up with none. Give God His 10 percent and end up with not 90 percent but 110 percent or more. Save your life and lose it. Losing it for His sake and for the gospel saves your life and builds His kingdom.

Money over family adds up to the strong possibility of *losing* both. Family over money assures the *security* of both. The most successful businessmen and businesswomen I know put their family first. They live by

Matthew 6:33 and prioritize the Lord Jesus and their sweet family above all.

I never knew a pastor who got a divorce because he lost his church. I've known several who lost their church because they got a divorce. *Family first.*

One Sunday morning I shared with my congregation the frustration of balancing family time and church responsibilities. I told them I had made the decision to put my family first. "I may not be at every committee meeting or church function," I said. "I may not make every hospital call or keep every appointment, but I will be at every little league game and school play and keep every date night with my wife."

And they stood and cheered!

Husbands, help your wife around the house. Anticipate her needs and meet them. Be thoughtful. Call if you're running late. Tell her how beautiful she is. Notice the little things she does. Silence the telephone. Get off the Internet and just enjoy being together. That's a wonderful woman you're married to. Get to know her. Be there. Hang out. Run errands together. Talk a lot. Laugh a lot. Marriage is great; enjoy it together!

I salute the working mom. I know tons of them who balance it all and get it right.

Jesus—number one. Family—number two. Job—way down on the list. And those unbelievably wonderful blessings God gave you called kids—love 'em, hug 'em, spank 'em, talk to 'em, play with 'em, brag on 'em. They'll be gone before you can blink an eye.

As kids get older, it gets easier to spend time together. They'll come more into your world, enjoy doing what you enjoy and want to do anyway. But while they're little, get down on their level. Get into their world. Watch cartoons with the kids, cut out paper dolls, play games, climb trees, play hide-and-seek, throw the football. And above all, be at their games, their school plays, and everything else important to them.

Don't let anything interfere with family time. Everything else can wait.

*He and all his family were devout
and God-fearing; he gave generously to
those in need and prayed to God regularly.*
ACTS 10:2 (NIV)

CHAPTER 25

WIN SOULS

L ast words are important and should be remembered. They sum up the person: who they were and what was important to them. In His last words on earth, Jesus said, "But ye shall receive power, after that the Holy Ghost is come upon you: and ye shall be witnesses unto me both in Jerusalem, and in all Judaea, and in Samaria, and unto the uttermost part of the earth" (Acts 1:8).

What we're to do: Be Christ's witnesses.

Where we're to do it: To the ends of the earth.

God has chosen to redeem the world through the redeemed. The Bible presents witnessing as a courtroom setting. Jesus Christ is on trial in every person's heart. The Devil is the prosecuting attorney: accusing Jesus, condemning Him. The Holy Spirit is the defense attorney: defending Jesus, commending Him. The evidence for Christ is overwhelming.

Internally. "There was a man sent from God, whose name was John. This man came for a witness, to bear witness of the Light, that all through him might believe. He was not that Light, but was sent to bear witness of that Light. That was the true Light which gives light to every man coming into the world" (John 1:6-9, NKJV).

Externally. "For the wrath of God is revealed from heaven against all ungodliness and unrighteousness of men, who suppress the truth in unrighteousness, because what may be known of God is manifest in them, for God has shown it to them. For since the creation of the world

His invisible attributes are clearly seen, being understood by the things that are made, even His eternal power and Godhead, so that they are *without excuse*" (Romans 1:18-20, NKJV, emphasis added).

Biblically. "Search the scriptures; for in them ye think ye have eternal life: and they are they which testify of me" (John 5:39).

Experientially. As the Holy Spirit tries the case for Christ, He knows which witness He needs and when. When He opens the door and calls on you, tell people what He's done for you. Give the testimony! Your witness is crucial to the outcome.

In 1972, Deacon Cy Perkins bolted from his seat in our choir, came trembling to the altar, and said, "Pastor, I've never been saved." Cy Perkins promised God he would never live another day without attempting to lead someone to Christ who may have "missed it" as well. He spent the last forty-six days of his life in a hospital bed. On day thirty-two, he wept. "Pastor, I'm so ashamed. I've only led twenty-three people to Christ since I've been here."

Search your soul and answer the question: "What is it about? What is it really about?" The purpose of these pages is not to shame you but to encourage you. I think I can help.

In John 2 there is an easy-to-miss key that makes being a witness the easy, natural, comfortable experience it was intended to be. Andrew is the gold standard for personal evangelism. He only made The Book three times, but all three times he's bringing someone to Jesus.

- Simon, who would become Peter the Rock (see John 1:40-42)
- The boy with the loaves and the fish (see John 6:8-9)
- The Greeks who said, "Sir, we would like to see Jesus" (see John 12:20-22)

Let's look at the technique of the master soul winner.

One of the two who heard John speak and followed Him, was Andrew, Simon Peter's brother. He found first his own brother Simon and said to him, "We have found the Messiah" (which translated means Christ). He brought him to Jesus. Jesus looked at him and said, "You are Simon the son of John; you shall be called Cephas." (John 1:40-42, NASB)

Three simple steps may easily be seen:

1. Rub shoulders with people. Andrew found his brother. Every day we find our brother. It may be knocking on doors, visiting prospects, or casual conversation in a secular setting. Finding our brother is social contact. Rubbing shoulders. Living life. And it happens every day.

2. Give your personal testimony. Andrew told his brother whom he had found: "We have found the Messiah." We've found Jesus; He's real. *Your personal testimony* of the One you have found and what He's done for you is the *irrefutable argument* for the Christian faith.

3. Bring them to Jesus. Andrew brought Simon to Jesus. We bring people to Jesus by presenting the plan of salvation and leading them in the sinner's prayer. And it's as easy as reading, "For all have sinned, and come short of the glory of God" (Romans 3:23); "For the wages of sin is death; but the gift of God is eternal life through Jesus Christ our Lord" (Romans 6:23); and "For whosoever shall call upon the name of the Lord shall be saved" (Romans 10:13).

We make it hard because we jump from number 1 to number 3.

Number 2, your *personal witness,* your own testimony, is the anesthetic that lets the gospel needle go in more easily. And you don't even have to find ways to bring up the subject. If you are attentive, many times a day as you're in casual conversation, the Holy Spirit will open the door for you to say something about Christ and what He means to you. You need only the courage to walk through the door and the sensitivity to know when it's open.

As you finish this chapter, I hope you do so with resolve in your heart: "I will do what I was called to do, what my Lord made so clear in those last words. I will be His witness. I will lead people to Jesus

Christ—personally." Nothing more authenticates our claim to be His
followers. Nothing more strongly encourages the journey.

The fruit of the righteous is a tree of life,
and he who wins souls is wise.

PROVERBS 11:30 (NIV)

CHAPTER 26

LET IT GO

J esus was misunderstood, falsely accused, rejected by His own, and
nailed to a cross.

Following in His steps, you cannot escape much of the same.
Unforgiveness and resentment can result. Anger and bitterness can
spread through your heart and soul like wildfire.

Very often the answer is to walk away. And it's just about that
simple if you can learn one little secret: It takes all your effort and
complete focus.

Paul had enough baggage for two men. We have recounted his perils
previously. Read his letters and hear his heart.

> *I don't mean to say that I have already achieved these things or that
> I have already reached perfection. But I press on to possess that perfec-
> tion for which Christ Jesus first possessed me. No, dear brothers and
> sisters, I have not achieved it, but I focus on this one thing: Forgetting
> the past and looking forward to what lies ahead, I press on to reach
> the end of the race and receive the heavenly prize for which God,
> through Christ Jesus, is calling us.* (Philippians 3:12-14, NLT)

Paul was not satisfied with who he was. He wanted more. Only
complete conformity to the image of the resurrected Christ would do.
His self-written prescription begins with six words: "I focus on this one

thing." I must bring all my emotional, mental, and spiritual faculties to bear on *one thing*—forgetting the past.

And just what is in the past? Only two things: good things and bad things. Obviously, we want to remember the good things. They bless, inspire, and encourage us.

It's the bad things that drag us down and set our feet in the concrete of yesterday—gossip, lies, misrepresentation, criticism, failure. It's reasonable to be bitter. It's also fatal. The stress of resentment and unforgiveness can kill you physically, emotionally, and spiritually.

It is well known that the tension of anger, rage, bitterness, and related types of stress releases the hormone cortisol into the bloodstream. Greatly increased levels of cortisol are highly toxic, contributing to high blood pressure, hardening of the arteries, stroke, or heart attack. Forgiveness greatly slows and even stops the flow of cortisol in the body.

Whoever it was, whatever they said, whatever happened, you've got to let it go.

Letting it go is a choice you make—not because it's easy but because it's necessary.

My dad and I were changing the marine battery in our boat when we accidentally dropped the good one overboard. He dove in after it. I waited for what seemed an eternity for him to emerge. When he came up empty-handed, I asked, "Why did it take so long to come up?" He told me he was doing everything he could to hold on to that battery, but it was too heavy and he finally had to let it go—or drown.

Human personhood is comprised of knowledge, emotion, and will. In our mind, we know we should turn it loose, let it go, forgive, and move on. But we tell ourselves, "He hurt me so bad," "I hate him so much," or "I can't forgive."

What are we saying? If we didn't feel this way, we could forgive. If we *felt* a certain way, we could *do* a certain thing. But forgiving is not an act of the *emotions*; it is an act of the *will*. Forgiveness is a choice you make, not because it *feels* right but because it *is* right.

And it is right. We can't incarnate the gospel of forgiveness and not forgive—not for a minute. We must *volitionally* choose to forgive and forget. Only then will emotional relief and release come.

No single volume, let alone a single chapter, could cite the devastating effects of unresolved resentment—physically, psychologically, emotionally, and spiritually.

But know this: You can never carry the banner of the gospel of forgiveness if you can't and won't forgive. In concluding His model prayer, which includes "as we forgive our debtors," Jesus went back and re-emphasized only one thing: "If ye forgive men their trespasses, your heavenly Father will also forgive you" (Matthew 6:12,14).

We're in the business of forgiveness. Let it go.

Get rid of all bitterness, rage, anger, harsh words,
and slander, as well as all types of evil behavior. Instead,
be kind to each other, tenderhearted, forgiving one
another, just as God through Christ has forgiven you.
EPHESIANS 4:31-32 (NLT)

CHAPTER 27

BE A GIVER

A few years ago, the newspapers were filled with the story of Carlos Rogers of the Toronto Raptors. Carlos had worked long and hard to get to the NBA. It was a dream come true. His future, everything he worked for, was in his hands. Now he was possibly throwing it all away. Why? Carlos's sister was sick. Very sick. She could not survive without a new kidney. Carlos Rogers was willing to leave the NBA to go home and donate one of his kidneys to his beloved sister. He knew it could end his career, but compared to his love for his sister, he didn't care. *USA Today* called Carlos Rogers "the most unselfish man in the NBA."

Be generous. Be a giver. While it may not be at the top of the list, your relationship to your earthly possessions is certainly an important indicator of the depth of your relationship with the Lord. Few things are more an extension of who we *are* than what we *have*. Our wealth represents our job, daily schedule, time, sweat, labor, and talents. They are indeed who we are. Our money is our house, utility bills, food and clothes, leisure, health care, and retirement. Our money is us.

It's not possible to be rightly related to Him and not be rightly related to our physical possessions. There are 2,380 verses in the Bible about money and our relationship to it. It is the number one topic of the parables. Second only to salvation, the stewardship of our possessions is the most prominent theme of the New Testament. More is said about our money and our possessions than prayer, faith, and hell combined.

Christianity is a cross, and a cross is "I" crossed out. If I've truly been to Calvary, so has my billfold. It is unthinkable that a servant of the One who gave His all is not a giving person.

And it's more than giving money. It's about giving your time, unconditional love, service, indeed your very life for others—and for Him. It's an attitude that says, *"The answer is yes. What's the question?"* The heart of the gospel is John 3:16. The heart of John 3:16 is *gave*. "For God so loved the world, that he *gave* his only begotten Son" (emphasis added). It is His nature to love. It is His nature to give. If He is ours and we are His, it will be our nature as well.

And it all begins with your tithe, right off the top, given to the church every Sunday.

Perhaps you're thinking, *But tithing is Old Testament, and grace is New Testament!* While that's true, it's also true that the New Testament goes beyond the Old Testament. Grace exceeds the law. Everything about it is *more* than, never *less* than.

Jesus asked in Matthew 5:47, "What do you do more than others?" (NKJV). Christianity is a *more than* religion. Grace always exceeds law. In everything Jesus ever said, taught, or did, He exceeded the law. Someone hit you? Turn the other cheek. Lost your shirt? Throw in your jacket. *More than! More than!*

For a Jew to give more under the law than a Christian under grace is a disgrace to grace. If our relationship to our possessions is an important indicator of the genuineness of our relationship to Him, then the *more than* principle definitely applies to everything we have.

"Give, and you will receive. Your gift will return to you in full—pressed down, shaken together to make room for more, running over, and poured into your lap. The amount you give will determine the amount you get back" (Luke 6:38, NLT).

Love God.

Be a giver.

At the end of the day, your cup will surely run over.

Blessed are those who are generous,
because they feed the poor.

PROVERBS 22:9 (NLT)

CHAPTER 28

LOVE PEOPLE

Some religions are religions of death. Our Christian faith is life. Some religions are religions of hate. Ours is love. Is there a sweeter word in the human vocabulary than *love*? God is love. His Son is the expression of His love, and we are the expression of His Son. One of the most important ingredients of staying power in the Christian life is a genuine God-given love for people. They are at once our greatest joy and greatest heartache, are they not?

God's love is unconditional, universal, and genuine. We can be no less in the work of His kingdom.

Loving those who love us back is the easy part. Loving those who hurt or dislike us is the hard part. How do we cultivate love for the hard to love?

Jesus addressed this very question in the parable of the unjust steward. The point of the story is that God's forgiveness of our ten thousand–talent debt was so great that we can ill afford not to forgive our neighbor's debt of one hundred pence. I think loving the unlovely begins with humility. I, too, am unworthy of love. If God could love me, the chief of sinners, He could love anyone and so must I (see 1 Timothy 1:16). To see ourselves as God sees us is to see others through His eyes.

I think it's important to learn to walk in someone else's shoes. The bitter, the critical, the negative—these people are what they are and think as they think for a reason. They are the product of a set of life situations, over many of which they've had no control whatsoever. They have been shaped and molded by other persons and the tough realities of life. Perhaps life has been better to me than to them. Perhaps my path has been lighted by encouragers, theirs by critics. Mine by love, theirs by hate. There, but for the grace of God, go I.

It helps to love people if we can look beyond who they are to who they can become. Abraham lied about Sarah, but through him was born the Savior of the world. Moses lost his temper in the wilderness but led the children of Israel out of it. Saul of Tarsus was the antagonist of the church; as the apostle Paul, he was its great protagonist. Who knows what the unlovely may become?

In 1972, my wife and I stepped off a plane to preach a citywide crusade in Lagos, Nigeria. One of the little boys who crowded around to carry our bags innocently tinkled on my foot. I hugged him, tipped him generously, and invited him to the crusade. Israel Akanji later became a Christian, a pastor, and president of the Nigerian Baptist Convention. God loved a little boy and saw what he could become. If we would truly love as He loved, we must do the same.

To love people is to get involved in their lives. The unlovable can become lovable when we demonstrate God's love toward them. Walk with them. Hurt with them. And listen, really listen to them. Hear what they *say* but, even more, what they're *saying*. Some of my dearest friends are precisely that because I took the time to get beyond their exterior and into their hearts.

People who see Christ's love in us are drawn to Him. How warm was the love of Ruth for her mother-in-law, Naomi. The bond of love in her heart far exceeded her love for her roots and culture. Who could ever forget her words?

Don't ask me to leave you and turn back. Wherever you go, I will go; wherever you live, I will live. Your people will be my people, and your God will be my God. Wherever you die, I will die, and there I will be buried. May the LORD punish me severely if I allow anything but death to separate us! (Ruth 1:16-17, NLT)

Ruth never found the one true God until she found His love in Naomi's life. Her testimony *"Your God will be my God"* speaks volumes of the Lord's genuine presence in the life of her mother-in-law. You are special to me because of who you are in Him and who He is in you. I want what you have. I want to be like you. I want to be with you. I love you. "Wherever you go, I will go."

A professor giving the final exam for a nursing degree said to his class, "I want to tell you up front that one of the questions will be worth 10 percent of your final grade: 'What is the name of the janitor who cleans your hallway?'"

The students protested, "That's not fair!"

He replied, "The profession you are entering is not just about shots and charts, thermometers and medications; it's about people."

The professor was right. It *is* all about people. Love people.

By this all will know that you are
My disciples, if you have love for one another.
JOHN 13:35 (NKJV)

CHAPTER 29

DO THINGS FIRST CLASS

Jesus aspired to excellence and obtained it. We must at least make it our goal.

The prize is perfection. We probably won't make that. Not here. But we do run the race toward the goal. And we run to win.

An effort of just okay is not worthy of Him.

I confess that almost everything comes easy for me — too easy. And that brings a lot of guilt. It is at once my pleasure and my Achilles' heel. The biggest temptation in my life is to "just slide through it." Just git 'er done and move on. But that's not good enough for Him. I am capable of more effort, more diligence. I could apply myself more. And that's a blessing and a curse.

At this writing, we're doing some remodeling on our home. You know, one contractor and lots of subcontractors, or subs.

Moments ago, my wife said, "You know, honey, none of them is really doing excellent work; they're all just pretty good."

How many times has our Lord looked down on His "subs" and said precisely the same thing? "Just okay" or "pretty good" is worthy of neither the Father who gave His Son nor the Son who gave His life for us.

The goal is excellence. Not perfection, but excellence. Pursue it.

Think above average. Care above average. Pray above average. Lead above average.

Romans 12:11 says it well: "Not lagging in diligence, fervent in spirit, serving the Lord" (NKJV).

In his commentary, William Barclay wrote of Romans 12:11: "Do not be sluggish in zeal. Keep your spirit at boiling point. How can we ever just be 'easy going' in anything we are or do for Him?"[5]

Solomon counseled, "Whatever your hand finds to do, do it with all your might" (Ecclesiastes 9:10, NIV).

When you fix someone's car, do it first class.

When you keep someone's books, do it first class.

When you landscape someone's yard, do it first class.

When you teach your Sunday school lesson, do it first class.

When you represent the King—when you live your life for Him—do it first class.

Soon after the Iron Curtain came down, I was privileged to be one of the first American pastors to preach in Russia. We held three citywide crusades, each packed out, with an overwhelming response. One night the pastors invited me to one of their homes for dinner. It was a very poor home. The house was immaculate but the furniture sparse, only the basics. The children's clothes, though starched and ironed, were very worn. The meal? Mashed potatoes. That's it. But it was the biggest and the best bowl of mashed potatoes I've ever had. Potatoes were the only food this family had to serve their guests, and they did so with excellence. They made the meal with class, for the Lord.

I've been in palaces and mansions. I've dined on prime rib, lobster, and pheasant under glass.

But the meal I shall never forget is the excellent mashed potatoes I ate in Russia.

First class.

Made with excellence.

For the King of kings.

That you may approve the things that are
excellent, that you may be sincere and
without offense till the day of Christ.
PHILIPPIANS 1:10 (NKJV)

Don't Play God

J esus said, "Whoever wants to be first must take last place and be the servant of everyone else" (Mark 9:35, NLT). Having by giving was a common theme in Jesus' teaching. Finding by losing. Living by dying. The way up is down.

This goes against our very nature, doesn't it? Something in us wants to be at the top of the heap; we want the very first place, not the last! Campus Crusade for Christ has a great phrase: "God loves you and has a wonderful plan for your life." The problem is that we, too, have a plan, and it's to get to the top—to be *the man* or *the woman.* Perhaps no greater temptation confronts us than self-promotion, and there are a hundred ways to do it.

After our church called my successor, I learned the majority of the letters of recommendation to our pastor search committee during those four and a half years came from men recommending themselves. The chairman of another search committee told me nearly 90 percent of their letters were self-recommendations. I didn't ask, but I'm fairly certain they were not pastors recommending themselves to smaller churches.

Why do we want prominence and celebrity? Because we want to be somebody, the leader of the parade, the king of the hill. It is in the DNA of our Adamic nature. Satan knows this, and that's why he wooed and tempted Eve to take a bit of the forbidden fruit with the words "You will be like God" (Genesis 3:5, NLT). But in between then and now, Jesus died on the cross to free us from our pride and selfishness. As we grow in Him, our sin nature should lessen and die. "He must increase, but I must decrease" (John 3:30).

Don't take Satan's bait. Don't be a self-promoter. God does have a wonderful plan for your life. It's a special plan and you don't want to spend one minute outside it.

God's good at putting it all together. Remember, He's never early or late; He's always on time. Romans 8:28 is still in the Bible and He's still got the "whole wide world in His hands." Let Him promote you. Let Him advance your life—at His pace.

Don't spend your life looking for greener pastures. Cultivate the one you already have. That's what God's faithful people do. You don't want to go where God doesn't want you to be. God has your phone number and knows your address with zip code.

Be God's man or God's woman right where you are. Don't spend your life looking over your shoulder. "All the days ordained for me were written in your book before one of them came to be" (Psalm 139:16, NIV).

Years ago, a dear pastor told me the following story.

In London during World War II, a little girl was praying one night before going to bed. She prayed for her mother and daddy, her friends, and her pet, and then she concluded, "And dear Lord, take care of Yourself because if anything happens to You, we're sunk."

Let God be God. He's really good at being God! And He still answers little girl's prayers.

"For I know the plans I have for you," declares
the LORD, "plans to prosper you and not to harm you,
plans to give you hope and a future."

JEREMIAH 29:11 (NIV)

CHAPTER 31

BE A SECOND-MILER

Citizens of occupied countries in the Roman Empire were required to carry the packs of Roman soldiers passing through their land for one mile.[6] Jesus said, "Carry them two."

Akron, Ohio, letter carrier Keith McVey is a hero to a lot of people. Over the years, McVey has helped save the lives of three people while on his mail route, earning the reputation as the humble superhero of his small neighborhood near a lake. In 2010, he threw aside his bundle of mail to perform CPR on an unconscious man on the side of the road. In 2008, he pulled a drowning girl from the lake. In 1990, when a teenager tried to take his life by jumping off a bridge on a snowy winter day, McVey, unable to stop him from jumping, covered the teen with blankets and helped keep him alive until an ambulance arrived. Keith McVey is a second-miler.[7]

The Sermon on the Mount is the constitution of the kingdom.

And the key verse is Matthew 5:17: "Do not think that I came to destroy the Law or the Prophets. I did not come to destroy but to fulfill" (NKJV).

What the law required, Jesus exceeded. His children do the same.

How can we do less? He held back nothing. He gave everything for us!

BC: "Why?"
AD: "Why not?"

BC: *"How much do we have to give?"*
AD: *"How much can we give?"*

BC: *"A whole mile?"*
AD: *"Only a mile?"*

Being a second-miler should be done with ease and grace, never with a view toward reward. My sweet wife and I have found that in the second mile are many second blessings.

Recently, the transmission went out in her car well after the warranty had expired. Her dealership went the second mile and replaced it anyway.

I sometimes think God has a special sense of humor as well as a special sense of timing.

Never give to receive. Never walk two miles for reward—any kind of reward.

Jesus' cross was many second miles beyond His throne. Do it because you're His and because you love Him. But get that umbrella out because there will be showers of blessings.

In 1984, our church bought land with a building and began to convert it into Louetta Road Baptist Church. The remodeling was eagerly begun by a team of twelve volunteers. Predictably, the project cost more and took longer than anticipated.

Night after night, weekend after weekend, our team of volunteers labored, wearied, and dropped out until only one faithful worker remained. Week after week, month after month, David Hill went the second mile—and finished the job—alone!

Today, Louetta Road is a healthy, growing church thanks to one humble carpenter who went the second mile—and more.

*When a woman who had lived a sinful life in that town
learned that Jesus was eating at the Pharisee's
house, she brought an alabaster jar of perfume, and as she
stood behind him at his feet weeping, she began
to wet his feet with her tears. Then she wiped them with
her hair, kissed them and poured perfume on them.*

LUKE 7:37-38 (NIV)

CHAPTER 32

EARN YOUR LEADERSHIP

Many analogies illustrate the relationship of Jesus and His people. Captain and soldier, master and servant, vine and branch, head and body. The ones I like best are bride and groom, used in Revelation, and husband and wife, used by Paul in Ephesians.

Ephesians 5:22 says, "Wives, submit to your own husbands, as to the Lord" (NKJV). Now that's far enough. You don't like it, right? If your answer is yes, read on.

Paul made clear that *leadership is earned not demanded.* "*Husbands, love your wives, just as Christ also loved the church*" (Ephesians 5:25, NKJV, emphasis added). And how was that? He *died* for the church. The apostle Paul doesn't say anything about the wife dying for her *husband.* The call is for the husband to die for his wife. The husband's honor to his wife, by the selfless pouring out of himself to serve her and bless her, is even *greater* than hers to him.

And what woman wouldn't be only too happy to honor such a husband as head of her home?

What athlete wouldn't honor such a coach?

What congregation wouldn't honor such a pastor as leader of the church?

What employees wouldn't honor an employer who treats them like that?

There's that Cross principle again. We always seem to come back here, don't we?

The honored and exalted women of the New Testament poured out their lives to minister to the apostle Paul and to the Lord Jesus in His life and at the tomb. But whether man or woman, business world or church, the concept is the same: Leadership is earned not demanded.

He who is greatest among you shall be your servant.

MATTHEW 23:11 (NKJV)

Submitting to one another in the fear of God. Wives, submit to your own husbands, as to the Lord. For the husband is head of the wife, as also Christ is head of the church; and He is the Savior of the body. Therefore, just as the church is subject to Christ, so let the wives be to their own husbands in everything. Husbands, love your wives, just as Christ also loved the church and gave Himself for her. . . . This is a great mystery, but I speak concerning Christ and the church.

EPHESIANS 5:21-25,32 (NKJV)

CHAPTER 33

MAXIMIZE INTEGRITY

It deeply hurts but it's deeply true: Loss of integrity has led to loss of respect for Christianity in America.

A man in a restaurant noticed the man seated at the table next to him was eating from many, many dishes of food. When asked why he had ordered so much, the man said he was testing everything on the menu. Asked why he was getting such special treatment, he smiled and said, "I'm in training to be a waiter, and I must taste everything on the menu because I can't recommend it to the customers unless I've tasted it first."

Sometimes integrity can be fun—when, like the waiter, your training involves tasting everything on the menu. However, training to be men and women of integrity isn't always enjoyable. Take Job, for instance.

> The LORD said to Satan, "Have you considered My servant Job? For there is no one like him on the earth, a blameless and upright man fearing God and turning away from evil. And he still holds fast his integrity, *although you incited Me against him to ruin him without cause.*" (Job 2:3, NASB, emphasis added)

Everywhere we look—politics, ministry, sports—it seems there is another embarrassment to the name of Christ. You can easily make your own list of fallen Christian celebrities. I need not drag their names through the mud, citing them again in these pages. They've suffered enough. My heart breaks for them.

There was a time when the world assumed Christian leaders were men and women of God. They had to prove they were not. Today they have to prove that they *are*.

And it's made every follower of Christ suspect, including you.

Here's my definition of *integrity*: "You do what people assume a Christian does when no eyes behold your behavior." You are what you appear to be. The inside matches the outside. You walk the talk, *whether or not anyone's taking notes.* If others could read your mind, they would be blessed not shocked. How is your integrity when you are:

- On the Internet?
- With a coworker?
- Paying your taxes?
- Out of town with friends or your family?
- All alone?

Joseph is a great example of integrity. He was a young, virile adult male with hormones raging, heart racing. His employer, Potiphar, was away on a trip. Servants were dismissed for the day, and Mrs. Potiphar and Joseph were alone. He was a virgin, handsome, and well-favored — we know. Mrs. Potiphar was a hottie — we assume. Probably a frustrated housewife who'd been watching too many "soaps." Give her credit for one thing though. She came right to the point: "Lie with me" (Genesis 39:7). Just as quickly and as automatic as tying his shoes in the dark came Joseph's response: "How then could I do this great evil and sin against God?" (Genesis 39:9, NASB). Joseph saw it coming, and he was ready.

We can't keep redetermining our values in every tempting situation. We need to settle that every morning when we are alone with God. I know lots of Christians who didn't make it all the way to the finish line. Smart, charismatic, cool, good-looking, sharp as a tack, but where are they now? I know many others who finished well. And I can tell you, whether famous or not-so-famous, there was one difference constant in them all: *integrity*.

Don't think for one minute that because your position of service is not prominent, what you do matters less. If you're a child of God, you're called to a life of integrity.

You may be a greeter at the door, a nursery worker, the president of your company, or the janitor at the office. Your influence is far wider than you can imagine.

Many eyes are on you. You are essential to the body of Christ. Don't sell your birthright for a mess of porridge. Don't compromise your integrity. Ever!

I recently consulted with a church whose pastor was not giving anything financially and was abusing the church credit card. When confronted, he was truly repentant, paid back the money, and sincerely promised total integrity in the future. The church was struggling with whether to allow him to continue serving. Their question to me was a difficult one: "Is the pastorate a place for on-the-job training in integrity, or is integrity a prerequisite to the pastorate?" Think about it. Whichever side you come down on, two important facts remain:

- The situation should have never happened in the first place.
- Don't ever let yourself be in the position where you're the one on trial.

Integrity means I do what I'm supposed to do. And it means *I also do* what I say *you should do*. Jesus taught integrity to His disciples. The scribes and Pharisees didn't get the memo.

Then Jesus spoke to the crowds and to His disciples, saying: "The scribes and the Pharisees have seated themselves in the chair of Moses; therefore all that they tell you, do and observe, but do not do according to their deeds; for they say things and do not do them. They tie up heavy burdens and lay them on men's shoulders, but they themselves

are unwilling to move them with so much as a finger."
(Matthew 23:1-4, NASB)

Nowhere is integrity more important than in the home. Children grow up thinking of God in terms of how they view their father. How are you training them? The impact is eternal.

Blessed are the pure in heart: for they shall see God.
MATTHEW 5:8

CHAPTER 34

REST AND RELAX

Jesus told His disciples, "Come aside by yourselves to a deserted place and rest a while" (Mark 6:31, NKJV). If Jesus needed to rest and relax, we need it more.

I once knew an evangelist who traveled and preached fifty-one weeks a year, every night, back to back. The great majority of those days, he preached two, three, and four times a day. Not to mention two or three of the seven nights at home between Christmas and New Year's. Then January 1 he was back on the road again. Predictably, he came apart.

Come aside and rest awhile, or you will too.

A dear pastor friend committed suicide. Years before, he had a serious emotional breakdown. "John," he said, "I never got over the pressure of Sunday." He never relaxed on Monday. Never took a day off—365 days a year.

Jesus always went into nature to refresh—outdoors, in the garden, to a quiet place. Do you need to refill your tank, rethink your life, unwind, nourish your soul, and rekindle the fire? If so, don't apologize, and take a much-needed vacation. And don't call work! The fifth year I was at First Baptist, the church gave me the entire summer off. I can't begin to describe the new life in my soul *and in the church* on September 1. Come aside and rest awhile.

Do what you like. Go where you want.

Whatever else you do:

- Include some physical activity.
- Have a complete change of pace.
- Do something completely unrelated to what you normally do.
- Do it in a complete change of scenery.
- Include your family in at least part of it.
- Include the Lord in all of it. The physical, mental, emotional, and spiritual are inseparable.
- Be sure to have some quiet time — some down time, alone time, just you and the Lord time.

In his classic book *Waiting on God*, Andrew Murray wrote,

And now, Lord, what wait I for? I scarce know or can tell; this only I can say — "my hope is in Thee." Can God furnish a table in the wilderness? He smote the rock that the water gushed out; can He give bread also? Can he provide flesh for His people? If they had been asked whether God could provide streams in the desert, they would have answered, "Yes. God has done it: He can do it again." But when the thought came of God doing something new, they limited Him; their expectation could not rise beyond their past experience, or their own thoughts of what was possible. Do let us be aware of limiting the Holy One of Israel in our very prayer. Let us believe that the very promises of God we plead have a divine meaning, infinitely beyond our thoughts of them. Let us believe that His fulfillment of them can be, in a power and abundance of grace, beyond our largest grasp or thought.[8]

Early-morning time with God should raise our expectancy, expand our vision, and excite our day, particularly in those days off. Praying and going to *play* is as important as praying and going to *work*. Somehow without the stress of the day, the vision deepens. A day off can be the most spiritual day of all. And when you do take a day off, slow down.

My friend Dottie Brewer spent a harried day rushing from this playground to that with her seven-year-old grandson. At their bedtime prayers, he said, "Granny, I'm so tired. You do the praying, and I'll just do the 'Yes, Lord' stuff."

When you look back at the end of your life, few things will seem as important as those special times of refreshing. Times of letting go, building up, getting ready to "bring it" again. Slow down!

This is what the Sovereign LORD, the Holy One
of Israel, says:"In repentance and rest is
your salvation, in quietness and trust is
your strength, but you would have none of it."

ISAIAH 30:15 (NIV)

CHAPTER 35

BE FAITHFUL

At the end of your life, only two words matter: *Well done*. That's all you want to hear. Nothing else matters—the status of your position at work, your income, the breadth of your fame, the accolades of your peers—just those two words.

Not "you set the record"; not "you wrote the song"; not "you reached the pinnacle"; not "you penned the books"; not "you were *the man*." Nothing else matters, just two words: *Well done!*

And to whom will these words be spoken? "His master replied, 'Well done, good and faithful servant! You have been faithful with a few things; I will put you in charge of many things. Come and share your master's happiness!'" (Matthew 25:21, NIV).

Reduced to simplest terms, faithful servants do what they are supposed to do and go where they are called—to the very end. Whether they have been given five talents, two talents, or one talent, it makes no difference. The Sarah Graham of whom you have never heard will hear the same *well done* as the Billy Graham the whole world acclaims if she was faithful to do all she could with what she had, where she was.

Five talents given—five talents faithfully used. "Well done!"

Two talents given—two talents faithfully used. "Well done!"

One talent given—one talent faithfully used. "Well done!"

It's true of the banker or baker, missionary or mother.

The megachurch pastor who fails will never hear those words. The country church pastor who is faithful will. As well as the faithful Sunday school teacher, and farmer. "Well done!" If in the deepest corner of your heart you long to hear "Well done,"

- Focus on Him.
- Rejoice in the criticism you endure for His sake.
- Don't get caught up in the numbers game.
- Don't think any small task is an unimportant task.
- Give the credit to others and the glory to God.
- Be grateful you have a place to serve in the marketplace and in the church.
- Whatsoever your hand finds to do, do it with all your heart.
- Keep a gentle spirit and a humble heart.
- Never wander far from the Cross.

It's not about you; it's all about Him. Your faithfulness means everything—it alone is your crown and your glory.

When you die, those who knew you will be glad they did and that you made a difference in their lives. When you live again, you'll hear the only two words that matter: "*Well done*, good and faithful servant. *Well done!*"

And never underestimate the potential of one act of faithfulness.

Each Sunday for thirty years, three committed laymen—Ed Bost, Frank Gerault, and Phil Ray—labored hours after church to reproduce and mail cassette tapes of our sermons. Each session ended with a prayer, "Lord, bless these tapes to the ends of the earth."

Years later, someone mailed something very special to our church (see page 117).

Faithfully serve where God has placed you with all the grace He has given you.

Now it is required that those who have been given a trust must prove faithful.

1 CORINTHIANS 4:2 (NIV)

By God's Grace
The Order
Servants of the King

(210) 493-1103

Episode 294
1999

The first time I was in a Northeastern province in a large country in Asia, I was forced to travel alone by foot. A man approached me with a happy look in his eyes and of a pleasant countenance. He spoke fair English and I was surprised by what he said. "Saab, (short for Sahib), Jesus Christ is my Savior and God." I asked him to please relate to me how that wonderful rebirth had happened. He said that some time before he had found a "broken" cassette tape on one of the streets in a large city. He had wound it up and taken it to a shop to be repaired.

"It was a message by a Rev. John Bisagno (I had to supply the proper pronunciation) of Houston, Texas. It gave the invitation to renounce all other gods and come to the Lord God of Heaven and earth through Jesus Christ. I repented of my sin, determined to follow Christianity. I always knew there had to be a way to God. That was the first time I knew that Jesus was the way."

I told him that the Spirit of God had put eternity into his heart. Many of the converts in Asia tell me the same thing.

We had tea together at a small roadside shop. After praying, he went singing along his way, headed north toward the large city. Encouraged, I walked south softly singing "The longer I serve Him the sweeter He grows. The more I love Him more love He bestows..."

Within 15 or 20 minutes, I heard a motorcycle coming behind me. Turning to look, I was dismayed to see, dead and being dragged by his feet, my new and late Christian friend. Some Hindus who had overheard our conversation did that foul deed. His joy and testimony had cost him his life. I am so happy that God had somehow found a way to bring that soul into the Kingdom. I'm sure that I will see him again in Heaven.

In Christ's Mercy,

Kemper

Kensington B. Cromwell

Priest

CHAPTER 36

SHOW HOSPITALITY

Hospitality is a beautiful gift of the Holy Spirit. And it's not just about baking the cake; it's making the one for whom you bake it feel like the most special person in the world.

Lydia had the gift of hospitality; she also believed in people. You have to believe in people to trust them. You have to trust people to invite them into your home. Lydia not only invited Paul, Silas, Timothy, and Luke into her home but also *strongly urged* them to be her guests.

> *One of those listening was a woman named Lydia, a dealer in purple cloth from the city of Thyatira, who was a worshiper of God. The Lord opened her heart to respond to Paul's message. When she and the members of her household were baptized, she invited us to her home. "If you consider me a believer in the Lord," she said, "come and stay at my house." And she persuaded us. . . .*
>
> *After Paul and Silas came out of the prison, they went to Lydia's house, where they met with the brothers and encouraged them. Then they left.* (Acts 16:14-15,40, NIV)

Lydia was a "more than" woman, a real second-miler. Inviting people into your home, sharing the gift of hospitality, may be the ultimate gesture of love and respect one can pay another. If it's real, it will drip from the ceiling, smile from the walls, and sing from the carpet.

My dear wife has a double portion of the gift of hospitality. People stop in our entryway, look around as though gripped by love, and say, "It feels so warm here." Her gifts of interior design and spiritual sensitivity unite in a décor that actually breathes the love of Jesus. I wish you could all visit our home (two at a time, please!).

The women who ministered to Jesus had the gift of hospitality—in His life, by the cross, at the tomb. And it's not just a woman's gift. Paul wrote, "If anyone wants to provide leadership in the church, good! But there are preconditions: A leader must be well-thought-of, committed to his wife, cool and collected, accessible, and hospitable" (1 Timothy 3:1, MSG).

Being hospitable doesn't mean being the best party planner on the block. It's an acceptance in your heart that shines through clearly. Hospitality doesn't require an elegant meal. It is an attitude: "Welcome to my world; I'm really glad you're here."

I can honestly say the highlight of our week is when we welcome friends into our home—a hurting pastor, a misguided teenager, a husband who's lost his way, a young pastor seeking direction, or a friend to watch football. And it always seems to be better received in the den, by the fireside.

Earlier we thought together about the importance of just *being you*. Never is that easier than in your own home, but the gift of hospitality, no matter where it happens, is a welcoming gift.

Welcome to my office.

Welcome to our luncheon appointment.

Welcome to my home.

Welcome to my heart.

Welcome to the kingdom.

Hospitality wears a smile. Hospitality is a moment of relaxation, of humor and fellowship. Hospitality is a spirit and atmosphere: "Welcome, friend. Come on in. Take off your coat and stay awhile." I know one day, in the literal presence of Jesus, the last thing on my mind will be to look at my watch and say, "I just remembered I have another appointment."

Few of us excel in *every* spiritual gift given to edify the body of Christ. All of us, however, *possess* each gift and should be developing all of them, including hospitality.

A few encouraging words on developing the gift of hospitality:

- Take others seriously.
- Don't take yourself too seriously.
- Don't be in a hurry.
- Be secure in Him.
- No pretense; just be yourself.
- Focus on the other person.
- Love people.
- Laugh and relax.
- Invite someone over for beans and cornbread. (How 'bout me?)

My wife and I were recently welcomed into a formal reception by pastor, presidential candidate, and author Governor Mike Huckabee. He made us feel like we were the celebrities in his home—feet propped up by the fireside. That's hospitality.

There was an estate nearby that belonged to Publius,
the chief official of the island. He welcomed us to his
home and for three days entertained us hospitably.
ACTS 28:7 (NIV)

CHAPTER 37

LIVE RIGHTEOUSLY

G overnor Felix was not a righteous man.

A few days later Felix came back with his wife, Drusilla, who was Jewish. Sending for Paul, they listened as he told them about faith in Christ Jesus. As he reasoned with them about righteousness and self-control and the coming day of judgment, Felix became frightened. "Go away for now," he replied. "When it is more convenient, I'll call for you again." He also hoped that Paul would bribe him, so he sent for him quite often and talked with him. (Acts 24:24-26, NLT)

The apostle Paul talked with the governor about righteousness, self-control, and the judgment to come. Why these three subjects? Because Felix was the epitome of what righteousness is not. To please the Jews, not to mention his Jewish wife, Felix imprisoned Paul for two years. Righteous people please God and succeed. People pleasers please other people and fail.

Felix knew the only way to get out of a Roman prison was to bribe the governor, so he tempted Paul by sending for him often. Deceitful people put possessions above integrity.

Righteous people put integrity above everything. Paul, being righteous, did not offer the hoped-for bribe.

Felix trembled *before* the truth. Paul had the courage to *tell* the truth. Unrighteous people are unstable and uncertain. Righteous people are secure in the truth—and in God.

Felix had two miserable years in the governor's mansion. Righteous Paul had two productive years in prison.

Paul was so convinced of the judgment to come that he lived in reverential fear of God. His respect for God led him to self-control and righteousness.

Positional righteousness through Christ makes us right before God. Experiential righteousness validates it before men and women. Governor Felix saw it in Paul and trembled.

Is there any better definition of *righteousness* than *doing* right because it *is* right?

Following after righteousness also means passionately running *from* unrighteousness. It's not either/or, it's both. It's the old adage, "Did the ball hit the bat or did the bat hit the ball?" The answer? Yes.

The apostle Paul repeatedly exhorted us to flee from unrighteousness (see 1 Corinthians 6:8; 10:14; 1 Timothy 6:4-11; 2 Timothy 2:22-24):

- Favoritism
- Idolatry
- Greed
- Unwholesome speech
- Pride
- Foolish arguments, which generate jealousy and strife
- Arguments from corrupt minds, deceptive about godliness and true riches

A rather exhaustive list of unrighteousness, wouldn't you say? You can't run *after* righteousness unless you are running *from* unrighteousness. A simple profile of a righteous person is someone who is:

- Respectful of others
- Humble
- Not argumentative
- Not a know-it-all
- Not deceived about what's really valuable in life
- Focused on the face of Jesus and keeps it ever before him

During my college days at Oklahoma Baptist University, I heard a story in chapel I will never forget. A woman visited her son at college. As she entered his room, her eyes swept across the walls, which were covered with more than a dozen suggestive pictures. Her heart was grieved, but she said nothing. Several days later, the mailman delivered a package to the young man. It was a gift from his mother—a beautifully framed picture of the head of Christ. Proudly the boy hung the picture on the wall above his desk. That night, before he went to bed, he removed the pin-up picture that hung closest to the face of Christ. The next day another picture was consigned to the wastebasket. Day after day the pictures began to disappear until only one remained: the picture of the Savior. Focusing on His beautiful face changes everything.

Lot was a righteous man. Enoch walked with God. Jesus said John the Baptist was the greatest man born of women.

Follow righteousness. Tenaciously pursue it—eagerly, breathlessly, wholeheartedly. First Timothy 6:12 says, "Fight the good fight of faith." We train for a fight. We sharpen our focus and discipline our bodies. The Christian life is an all-out war, and it's got to be won. It's no side issue; it *is* the issue.

Pay the price.

Fight the fight.

Run the race.

Win the battle.

Be victorious.

Gain the prize.

Finish. Finish well! Finish strong!

The key is pursuing righteousness. Win the crown for Him. Engraved on it will be just two words: *Well done.* Follow after righteousness. It's worth the effort. Make Jesus look really good.

Dear children, don't let anyone deceive you
about this: When people do what is right, it shows
that they are righteous, even as Christ is righteous.

1 JOHN 3:7 (NLT)

CHAPTER 38

GROW CONSISTENTLY

We can't be perfect, but we do need to be headed in that direction.

There are three stages in the Christian life: justification, sanctification, and glorification.

> And we know that all things work together for good to those who love God, to those who are the called according to His purpose. For whom He foreknew, He also predestined to be conformed to the image of His Son, that He might be the firstborn among many brethren. Moreover, whom He predestined, these He also called; whom He called, these He also justified; and whom He justified, these He also glorified.
> (Romans 8:28-30, NKJV)

Notice the apostle Paul speaks of the singular *purpose* of God, not the many *purposes* of God. What is that one purpose? *To be conformed into the image of His Son.*

When we truly repent of our sin and receive Him as our Savior, we are born *all over again.* We are in a state the Bible calls justification. I have been justified in the sight of God, *just-as-if-I* had never sinned. Because I am clothed in His imputed righteousness, God views me as completely perfect in the righteousness of His Son. "For God made Christ, who never sinned, to be the offering for our sin, so that we could be made right with God through Christ" (2 Corinthians 5:21, NLT).

Justification is the first stage. Glorification is the third and final stage. When we see Jesus, we shall be like Him.

> *Beloved, now we are children of God; and it has not yet been revealed what we shall be, but we know that when He is revealed, we shall be like Him, for we shall see Him as He is.* (1 John 3:2, NKJV)

> *It will happen in a moment, in the blink of an eye, when the last trumpet is blown. For when the trumpet sounds, those who have died will be raised to live forever. And we who are living will also be transformed.* (1 Corinthians 15:52, NLT)

Stage 1: We have been justified. Stage 3: We will be glorified.

Between the day we were saved (justification) and the day we shall be transformed into His image (glorification), we are in the second stage, called sanctification. We are slowly but continually being made more and more holy, more Christ-like every day. To be sanctified is to be "holified."

Progress is happening on the road to glorification, to Christ-likeness. Each moment, each day, we are becoming less like us, more like Him.

Sanctification is not the goal. It is the process toward the goal. Glorification is the goal. Day by day, to be more like the Master. Regardless of our progress on the road to glorification, it will be instantly completed in a moment, in the twinkling of an eye, when we see Him face-to-face. Only then will we fully "be like Him."

We are a work in progress, growing consistently. Initially created in His image, ultimately re-created into His image.

Day by day, we are being conformed to the image of His Son. What a gold standard for God's children! But how do we achieve this?

What you *do* is important in the pursuit of holiness. Pursue prayer, Bible reading and study, worship, stewardship, fellowship, witnessing, charity, and more.

But equally important is our reaction to things that happen *to* us, things over which we have no control.

When God sees us at the moment of our justification, He views us as a master sculptor envisions an image in a block of marble. Somewhere down in there is what He wants to create — the image of His Son.

God must surely say, "I have such a long way to go!" So He takes the chisel of trials and the hammer of adversity and begins to chip away. He puts us in situations that cut away one unChrist-like quality after another. When we learn the lesson and progress is made, He moves on to another. And He *will* tell us the purpose of the trial.

> *Dear brothers and sisters, when troubles come your way, consider it an opportunity for great joy. For you know that when your faith is tested, your endurance has a chance to grow. So let it grow, for when your endurance is fully developed, you will be perfect and complete, needing nothing.*
>
> *If you need wisdom, ask our generous God, and he will give it to you. He will not rebuke you for asking.* (James 1:2-5, NLT)

Wisdom about what? The purpose of the trial.

Perhaps your most unChrist-like quality is your lack of faith. You just can't trust God. He may take away every means of financial support until you can do nothing *but* trust Him. No salary. No credit. No bank loan. Now that's a trial.

A trial has no escape clause. A trial is something you go through until His purpose is completed. Mission accomplished. What's next?

Some tourists were watching a miner pan for gold in Colorado. He turned the fire higher and higher beneath the cauldron, skimming off more and more dross. "How do you know when it's finished?" they asked. The miner responded, "When I can see the reflection of my own image, that's when I turn off the heat."

In the process of sanctification, there will be heat. But His grace is sufficient. Nowhere is it better said than in 1 Corinthians 10:13: "There hath no temptation taken you but such as is common to man: but God is faithful, who will not suffer you to be tempted above that ye are able, but will with the temptation also make a way to escape, that ye may be able to bear it."

The word *escape* does not capture the full meaning of the Greek. The idea is the enablement of endurance to go through the trial victoriously, without failing the test.

To grow consistently, to grow in grace, is to be moving along the road of sanctification toward complete Christ-likeness. The question is not "Are we there yet?" The question is "Are we on the bus?" If you're on the bus moving forward, don't get off. Keep going. Keep growing.

Honestly face the question "Am I growing?" Not in numbers, but in quality. Not my church—me. Not my income—me. What is your answer?

The way you run the race determines whether you finish the race. Keep growing, passionately and consistently. And you don't have to tell a soul. They'll notice.

But grow in grace, and in the knowledge
of our Lord and Saviour Jesus Christ.
To him be glory both now and for ever. Amen.

2 PETER 3:18

CHAPTER 39

PRAY EARLY

I can't speak for anyone else, but I can speak from my heart—for me. As I look back across sixty years of ministry, I see one common denominator in those seasons where everything was going especially well: *consistent early-morning prayer.*

And it's a very old and revered practice.

> *The next morning Jacob got up very early. He took the stone he had rested his head against, and he set it upright as a memorial pillar. Then he poured olive oil over it.* (Genesis 28:18, NLT)

If I have a day too full for early-morning prayer, it will take me twelve to fifteen hours to get through it. If I give God the first hour, He goes before me and smoothes the way and solves many problems before I get there. Then it takes only six to eight hours to get through the *same* issues of the *same* day.

> *But you will not even need to fight. Take your positions; then stand still and watch the LORD's victory. He is with you, O people of Judah and Jerusalem. Do not be afraid or discouraged. Go out against them tomorrow, for the LORD is with you!* (2 Chronicles 20:17, NLT)

Early-morning prayer puts God first; then He puts you first. You don't accomplish by doing, as much as by turning loose. There's that

Cross principle again. Living by dying, keeping by letting go, accomplishing by letting Him accomplish.

The Cross is the heart of the gospel. Matthew 6:33 is the heart of living it out: "But seek ye first the kingdom of God, and his righteousness; and all these things shall be added unto you."

Early-morning prayer says, "You're first." Early-morning prayer means quiet, solitude, silence, and peace. In the early hours, my mind is clear. My thoughts are uncluttered. Complex pictures clarify. Compound problems simplify. Peace in my heart means peace in my world.

Early-morning prayer tends more to listening than speaking. "Be still, and know that I am God" (Psalm 46:10).

God speaks more clearly in the garden of silence than on the busy corner of Third and Main. Life can drown out His voice, His still small voice. It's not a noisy, big voice; it's a whisper, an impression, a thought. And it's a game changer.

Our favorite early-morning prayer spot is our patio. Uldine has transformed it into a prayer garden. Two engraved stone plaques are beautifully placed among the flowers. One says, "Be still and know that I am God." The other, "Peace."

> *I come to the garden alone*
> *While the dew is still on the roses.*
> *And the voice I hear falling on my ear*
> *The Son of God discloses.*
>
> *And He walks with me, and He talks with me*
> *And He tells me I am His own.*
> *And the joy we share as we tarry there*
> *None other has ever known.*[9]

Listen. Just listen . . . can you hear Him?

In the early morning, while it was still dark,
Jesus got up, left the house, and went away to a
secluded place, and was praying there.
MARK 1:35 (NASB)

CHAPTER 40

DEMONSTRATE MEEKNESS

Longsuffering, forbearance, gentleness, love, peace, truth. These are not weak words; they are strong words. Meekness is not weakness. Meekness is strength under control. Remember well those words: *strength under control.*

James 3:2-3 says, "We get it wrong nearly every time we open our mouths. If you could find someone whose speech was perfectly true, you'd have a perfect person, in perfect control of life. A bit in the mouth of a horse controls the whole horse" (MSG).

Our tongues are like wild horses. God made us this way. The question is what to do with the wild horses of human nature. Hedonism would tell us to open the gates and let the wild horses run loose. Be number one. Look at me. Step on everybody, but get to the top. Do your own thing. If it feels good, do it.

If hedonism would release the wild horses of human nature, hyper-fundamentalism would beat them half to death until they're nothing but an old plug horse, pulling a milk cart down the back alleys of life. It's very much like the mother who heard her little boy playing in the garage and hollered, "Tommy, I don't care what you're doing; whatever it is, *stop it.*" Neither philosophy is akin to the character of the Nazarene.

Jesus is not *at war* with human nature. He would not berate our every trait 'til at last we whimper in the corner like a scolded puppy. Jesus is in the business of *fulfilling* human nature. Bridle and harness the wild horses. Put bits in their mouths and *ride them.*

Then you will go just as fast and just as far, but when you harness the wild horses for the kingdom, you'll be going somewhere. Your life will be fulfilled and His kingdom expanded. Let me say it again: *Meekness is not weakness. Meekness is strength under control.*

Some may say, "My problem is temper. I need to crush my temper and totally annihilate it." But I wish more people had a temper. More of us need to get angry at things worth getting mad about—the liquor traffic, the drug pusher, the smut peddler, the gang lord, and prejudice and injustice. Jesus had a temper, but it was under control. He didn't *lose* His temper; He *used* it. He harnessed it. It was *strength under control.* Blessed are the meek, not the weak!

The moneychangers in the temple were shortchanging people—good, devout people who had come at great effort and financial sacrifice to Jerusalem from across the Roman Empire. The temple tax had to be paid in Jewish money, and they had no idea how that translated into *their* money. They were being shortchanged in the very house of God.

The problem was not selling CDs in the lobby of the church. The problem was ripping off the customers in the process. And Jesus sat there, under control, slowly, patiently weaving a whip. Then He used it. He was never stronger, more dynamic, than in this hour. Weakness? Hardly. But strength! *Strength under control!* His anger was not *out of* control; it was fully *under* control. His control—in His time, in His way.

Meekness means you:

- Keep your cool.
- Hold your tongue.
- Bide your time.
- Control your emotions.
- Wait your turn.
- Act forcefully but gently.

- Speak softly but authoritatively.
- Harness the wild horses and ride them for His glory.

Meekness always holds something in reserve. It's got it all, but it's got it all under control. Meekness always has more in the storeroom than in the window, more in the tank than in the accelerator, more on the bench than in the game. And meekness always wins the game.

Blessed are the meek: for they shall inherit the earth.

MATTHEW 5:5

CHAPTER 41

BE BOLD

To be bold is not to be loud, offensive, or obnoxious. It's to be coura-geous, confident, unafraid to act, unafraid to speak the truth in love. To be bold is to trust in God's faithfulness when no one else believes. To be bold is to stand alone, if necessary. Unwavering, solid as a rock. Boldness is anchored in security and security in knowing "I stand on His promises—in His Word—and in His will."

Boldness is not brash and crass. It's unmovable and unwavering, but it's got a heart full of grace.

Adrian Rogers, pastor and three-term president of the Southern Baptist Convention, was the gold standard of boldness. Smart, prepared, secure, and *right*! And he was that in every issue I ever heard him defend and every stand I ever saw him take.

His sermons were strong, his convictions unwavering. But there was always a lilt in his voice, a smile on his face, and love in his heart. His secret was Peter and John's secret. Their boldness was for one reason and one alone: They had been with Jesus. Jesus was both bold and tender, the embodiment of love and discipline.

Adrian Rogers was bold as a lion and as gentle as a lamb. He was the real deal. He lived the life and walked the talk. Adrian had been with Jesus.

The Jesus I know was bold. He confronted the Pharisees. He got in the face of the Sadducees. Yet little children danced at His feet. And hurting people ran to His gentle touch. Jesus was both *bold* and tender. Great Christians always are. If they've been with Jesus, they'll be like Him.

To be bold is to speak what is true and to say what is right, not what is politically correct. To be bold is to stand before the tank in Tiananmen Square.

If they change the law and forbid you to condemn the sin of homosexuality from the pulpit or else you'll lose your church's tax exemption, what will you do?

Our city no longer has a Christmas parade; now it's called a holiday parade. There's no more "Merry Christmas," only "Happy Holidays." Perish the thought that the United States of America would have the audacity to mention the name of Jesus, the One who birthed her, sustains her, and protects her to this very hour!

Will you speak it the next time you lead in prayer at a secular gathering? Or will you say what is politically correct, what someone says you must say? If you've been with Jesus, I think you know the answer.

Be bold! You don't have to be brash or loud. Being bold comes from a deep-seated peace that you know His will and are standing in it. And that comes from a surrendered heart, saturated in His Word.

And it may cost you everything. Yes, they crucified Jesus, but remember who *they* were, and be bold.

For which I am an ambassador in chains;
that in proclaiming it I may speak
boldly, as I ought to speak.
EPHESIANS 6:20 (NASB)

CHAPTER 42

HONOR THE MANTLE

The mantle is the earliest symbol of divine authority and spiritual leadership.

He took the cloak that had fallen from [Elijah] and struck the water with it. "Where now is the LORD, the God of Elijah?" he asked. When he struck the water, it divided to the right and to the left, and he crossed over. (2 Kings 2:14, NIV)

"Consider now, for the LORD has chosen you to build a temple as the sanctuary. Be strong and do the work."
Then David gave his son Solomon the plans for the portico of the temple, its buildings, its storerooms, its upper parts, its inner rooms and the place of atonement. (1 Chronicles 28:10-11, NIV)

After the death of Moses the servant of the LORD, the LORD said to Joshua son of Nun, Moses' aide: "Moses my servant is dead. Now then, you and all these people, get ready to cross the Jordan River into the land I am about to give to them—to the Israelites." (Joshua 1:1-2, NIV)

Still worn in many traditions, the mantle is a symbol of great honor and respect. It is highly unlikely that your service for Him is the first of its kind. In all likelihood, someone else paved the way, pioneered the project, and laid the foundation on which you build. If Jesus tarries, someone else will just as certainly carry it on after you.

Mantles have two sides. The front speaks of those who follow after:

- From Elijah to Elisha—a power to be experienced
- From David to Solomon—a building to be completed
- From Moses to Joshua—a land to be possessed

The back of the mantle speaks of honoring those who have gone before:

- Elisha wanted the anointing Elijah had. Twofold.
- Solomon wanted to build the temple of which his father, David, only dreamed.
- Joshua encouraged the people to follow Moses' example and obey his commandments.

And what of David, the man after God's own heart, and his predecessor, King Saul?

In spite of the fact that Saul spared the Amalekites he was commanded to destroy, in spite of the fact that he offered an illegitimate sacrifice, in spite of the fact that he sought to kill David out of jealousy, David honored the mantle.

Upon Saul's death, David called him "the beauty of Israel" and praised him for his relationship with his son Jonathan (see 2 Samuel 1:19).

As Paul saw when he stood before the high priest, the position transcended the person.

It takes a big person to honor those who have gone before and acknowledge that you are building on their foundation.

Upon my retirement from First Baptist Church Houston, Gregg Matte became my successor. He is the most gracious, genuinely humble, wise young leader I know. These eleven years later I can't get him to stop acknowledging our presence when my wife and I attend our church.

Upon completion of my yearlong interim at the wonderful Colonial Heights Baptist Church in Greater Jackson, Mississippi, the new pastor insisted on making my last Sunday his first Sunday. In one of the most generous gestures of respect I've ever seen, he sat in the congregation that day rather than taking his pulpit. Pastor Jimmy Meek honored the mantle. Pastor Meek lived up to his name.

The mantle faces both directions. Sadly, many pastors, politicians, and other leaders criticize their predecessor. And too many others criticize their successor. When you're through, you're through. You had your turn; move on. Do everything in your power to guarantee the success of the one who follows you. Pass the baton and leave. Honor the mantle. I think the Golden Rule applies here. And that's at the office or at the church.

My last Sunday, I told the people that my wife and I would forever remain part of the church but we would not be back until several months after the new pastor had settled in. I wanted him to feel secure with his new congregation. Pastors shouldn't meddle in their church's affairs or decisions after they leave. Nor should you—in your organization, company, institution, or ministry. You've had your turn. Move on.

Only hours ago, I came from the fiftieth anniversary celebration of Houston Baptist University. Former president George W. Bush was the speaker, and he said, "I refuse to criticize my successor."

Render to all what is due them: tax to
whom tax is due; custom to whom custom;
fear to whom fear; honor to whom honor.
Romans 13:7 (NASB)

CHAPTER 43

STAY ON FOCUS

Finish the course. Stay on game. Keep on track. Stay on point. A thousand side issues, secondary matters, and time-consuming causes will clamor for your attention. All good, all worthy, but all siphoning off time and energy from the best. So, focus on the prize. Along with the apostle Paul say,

> I'm not saying that I have this all together, that I have it made. But I am well on my way, reaching out for Christ, who has so wondrously reached out for me. Friends, don't get me wrong: By no means do I count myself an expert in all of this, but I've got my eye on the goal, where God is beckoning us onward—to Jesus. I'm off and running, and I'm not turning back. (Philippians 3:12-14, MSG)

Focus. That's what makes a champion. First things first.

One of my friends is a high school dropout and a multimillionaire. He has the biggest heart for the Lord of any man I know and the *gift of giving* beyond measure.

I recently asked him, "How many financial appeals for Christian causes do you receive a year?"

He said, "About two or three a day."

"How do you handle it?" I asked.

"Well, after much prayer, the Lord and I came to an understanding," he said. "Rather than helping a lot of folks a little bit, I will invest my money in my church and three other worthy causes—and help a lot!"

Finishing strong means keeping the main thing the main thing. You must identify your magnificent obsession and pursue it exclusively, and sometimes that means having to "just say no."

The need to please can dull your focus and diminish your desire to win. I'd love to be all things to all men, but I guess I'll have to leave that one to the great apostle.

Just this week I received a manuscript from a dear pastor friend in California. It broke my heart to tell him I was behind on my own writing schedule and could not take time to read and write an endorsement for his new book. The bad part is, it hurt. The good part is, I stayed on focus.

Before taking on anything, ask yourself, "Does it maximize the goal and expand the part of the kingdom that God has called me to build, whether at my job or my church?" Successful people are focused people. They are on message, on game.

I always tell young pastors, "People aren't an *interruption* to your ministry; they *are* your ministry." But how do you balance the tender with the target? That's the kicker, and it's a stinger in the heart of this shepherd, or any caring follower of the Shepherd of Galilee. No single formula can direct you. No well-intended person can guide you. You will have to make your own choices and find your own balance. The Holy Spirit will be your guide, but sometimes you will have to gently say no. When you do, try to suggest someone else to help. You may be surprised to find how many people are waiting to help.

One Sunday morning I made a special appeal for people to work on an important project. Few responded. After the benediction, a man said, "Pastor, I didn't come forward today, but if you ever pick up the phone and personally ask me to do something for you, I will never turn you down." Staying on focus can mean narrowing the focus and being specific if you're going to hit the target.

Paul got it right. Paul finished well. He had the wisdom and found the grace to "just say no."

"This one thing I do" (Philippians 3:13).

———————————

But you, Timothy, man of God: Run for your life from all this. Pursue a righteous life—a life of wonder, faith, love, steadiness, courtesy. Run hard and fast in the faith. Seize the eternal life, the life you were called to, the life you so fervently embraced in the presence of so many witnesses.

1 TIMOTHY 6:11-12 (MSG)

CHAPTER 44

BE GRACIOUS

Long after they've forgotten what you did, they will remember what you were. You may disagree, you may not conform, you may have to be firm—but you can always be gracious. No nicer compliment will ever be paid you than this: "He was such a gracious person." "She was such a gracious lady." *Gracious*, of course, comes from the word *grace*. It's the heart of our Bible, the soul of our life. As in all things, Jesus is at once our example and our source: "Ye have tasted that the Lord is gracious" (1 Peter 2:3).

To experience His touch is to experience His grace—undeserved, imputed love. It softens the spirit, humbles the heart, and makes tender the personality and spirit of a child of the King. I deserve nothing, I can do nothing, I am nothing apart from His amazing grace. Somehow that translates to an elevated opinion of others and greatly affects the way I treat them:

- Courteously
- Politely
- Gently
- Tactfully
- Thoughtfully
- Obligingly
- Sometimes silently
- Always graciously

Gracious people recognize God's graciousness to them and pass it along to others, as when Jacob gave Esau flocks of sheep and herds of cattle when he went to make peace with his brother. He told Esau, "'Please, take my blessing that is brought to you, because God has dealt graciously with me, and because I have enough.' So he urged him, and he took it" (Genesis 33:11, NKJV).

Being gracious holds back harshness and payback. Graciousness overlooks wrong and extends love. "The LORD is merciful and gracious, slow to anger, and plenteous in mercy" (Psalm 103:8).

And it's beautiful in the lives of His people. "A gracious woman retains honor" (Proverbs 11:16, NKJV).

A woman of grace is a person of charm and class. The heart touched by His grace is that and much, much more. "He touched me"—and I can never again be the same.

"The words of a *wise man's* mouth are gracious" (Ecclesiastes 10:12, emphasis added). Wisdom is inseparably linked to a gracious heart.

Wisdom knows the difference between insight and judgmentalism. Wisdom discerns the intent of the heart. A harsh act can come from a remorseful heart. Wisdom knows when to speak strongly and when to speak redemptively.

And that means toward everyone—the jailer and the inmate, the doctor and his receptionist, the banker and her janitor, the governor and his driver.

Gracious words reflect one's upbringing and heritage. Good parents invest in their children a balance of justice and mercy, discipline and grace. They understand the importance of boundaries and second chances.

Most assuredly, Joseph and Mary were well recognized in Nazareth as great parents. The town "wondered at the gracious words which proceeded out of his mouth. And they said, Is not this Joseph's son?" (Luke 4:22).

Ungracious people are too self-centered to be courteous, polite, and thoughtful. They are never obliging to others. Self-centered people can't represent well the most selfless person who ever walked the face of the earth.

"For the LORD your God is gracious" (2 Chronicles 30:9).

Gracious and more. Much more! I couldn't begin to name the people I've met in life. Most only once, only for a moment.

Some rich.

Some influential.

Some glamorous.

Some powerful.

I remember most readily those who were gracious.

Nevertheless for thy great mercies' sake
thou didst not utterly consume them, nor forsake them;
for thou art a gracious and merciful God.
NEHEMIAH 9:31

CHAPTER 45

BE EXEMPLARY

Hall of Famer Bart Starr of the Green Bay Packers regularly sent encouraging notes to his son in middle school. Each note had a dime taped to it and ended with the words, "I really believe in you. Love, Dad."

One Sunday afternoon in St. Louis, Bart Starr had the worst game of his career. He threw three interceptions and almost single-handedly lost the game. He arrived home late that night and found a note on his dresser. It said, "Dad, I watched you play today. Wanted you to know, I really believe in you. Love, Bart Jr." Taped to the bottom of the note was a dime.

This chapter is written as a confession. Looking back, I see that I knew to do better than I did. I can't think of an area of my life where I was the man I wanted to be, let alone knew I should be. I long since took down the "I've got it made" plaque and put up the "Oh wretched man that I am" plaque. Somehow, the faster I go, the behinder I get. But to fellow strugglers I can say, along with you, I tried — and I'm still trying.

Where in any of our lives is there perfection? Where is the heart that can truly say, "Do as I do"? Paul said, "Be imitators of me, just as I also am of Christ" (1 Corinthians 11:1, NASB).

Perhaps acknowledging that is the first step on the road to an exemplary life. I think you know the drill. My prayer is to help you execute it.

Perhaps the best motivation would be to look a bit more deeply at why it's important.

Jesus said, "You are the salt of the earth" (Matthew 5:13, NKJV).

He didn't say what you *do* is the salt or what you *preach* is the salt; He said, "*You* are the salt." Who you are makes all the difference.

You *will* impact your society, your culture, and your world. You may be strong salt or weak salt, but your very presence—weak or strong, tasteless or tangy—makes a difference one way or the other. Your facial expression, haughty air, critical attitude, negative spirit, lustful look, or prejudiced contempt gives off vibes with or without words. You—salty or tasteless, worthy or worthless, on the dinner table or on the road-bed—are still the salt of the earth.

Ever notice how some people can enter a room and be a brightener or a downer? Your presence makes a difference, so be an example.

It matters at church. The kids in your Sunday school class probably learn more about Christ-likeness, or lack thereof, from being around you one week at camp than they do from the Sunday school lessons you teach them all year long.

Your salt matters—big time!

It matters at home. The apple doesn't fall far from the tree. I've never known one boy who didn't have much of his father in him, or a girl much of her mother. And here's the scary part: Children grow up thinking of God in terms of how they think of their father—present or absent, gentle or tough, tender or mean, forgiving or unrelenting.

You're salt. Be good salt. Be an example in your church, in your home, in your world. Who first said, "I'd rather see a sermon than hear one any day"? Many times I have preached in the church of a pastor I didn't know. But the one thing I did know was that if he'd been there five years or more, his church would be just like him. If he was tough, I could expect no smiles, no joy from the congregation. If he was gentle and loving, I could expect lots of smiles and hugs, great singing, and a beautiful, happy spirit.

Be exemplary. It's important, more important than you know.

You're the only Bible a lot of people will ever read. The only Jesus they will ever know. Be exemplary.

Somebody's watching.

———

For I have given you an example,
that you should do as I have done to you.

JOHN 13:15 (NKJV)

CHAPTER 46

LIVE EXPECTANTLY

Out of sight? Yes. But out of mind? Never. With all my heart, I really do want Him to come quickly. The second coming of Christ is as real to me as life itself. It is the one event toward which all of history is moving, and without which, none of history makes any sense.

He came the first time to die here.
    He's coming the second time to dictate here.
He came the first time to board here.
    He's coming the second time to be boss here.
He came the first time to be resident.
    He's coming the second time to be president.

One in every twenty-seven verses in the New Testament refers directly or indirectly to the second coming of Jesus Christ. That motivates me in three ways:

1. My time is short. My world is needy. My friends are lost. I must work—work fast, work faithfully, work hard. "We must work the works of Him who sent Me as long as it is day; night is coming when no one can work" (John 9:4, NASB).

In Matthew 24, Jesus gave many signs of His return. In verse 33 He said, "So likewise ye, when ye shall see all these things, know that it is near, even at the doors."

Many of these signs have happened before. Some in one season, some in another. But Jesus said the time will come when these signs will be happening simultaneously. "When ye *shall* see [present tense] all these *things* [plural], know that it is near, even at the doors" (Matthew 24:33, emphasis added). And that time is now. Right now. Live expectantly.

2. My purity is precious. God has given me the beautiful gift of an adoring family, faithful friends, and an expanding opportunity to serve. I must not and will not fail Him. Holiness and purity are inseparable from usefulness. What do I want to be doing when Jesus returns? Will I be embarrassed, or will I be blessed?

I'm dead serious about that. "In a moment, in the twinkling of an eye, at the last trump: for the trumpet shall sound, and the dead shall be raised incorruptible, and we shall be changed" (1 Corinthians 15:52). Live expectantly. Make every decision against the backdrop of this question: Do I want to be doing this when Jesus returns? "Beloved, now we are children of God, and it has not appeared as yet what we will be. We know that when He appears, we will be like Him, because we will see Him just as He is. *And everyone who has this hope fixed on Him purifies himself,* just as He is pure" (1 John 3:2-3, NASB, emphasis added).

3. My faithfulness is a treasure. Think on this: Suppose I serve Christ thirty-five years, give it up, go back into the world, and He comes thirty-five years and one month after I started serving Him. So near, yet so far.

I want to be found faithful to the very end, right up until the second He calls me home. Now that makes me smile.

Live expectantly.

For as the lightning cometh out of the east,
and shineth even unto the west; so shall
also the coming of the Son of man be.
MATTHEW 24:27

CHAPTER 47

INITIATE RECONCILIATION

William Barclay wrote,

To be effective, sacrifice would have to include confession of sin and true penitence: and true penitence involves the attempt to rectify any consequences sin might have had. Not even the sacrifices of the Day of Atonement could avail for a man unless he was first reconciled to his neighbor. The breach between man and God can not be healed until the breach between man is healed. The Jews were quite clear that a man had to do his utmost to put things right himself before he could be right with God.[10]

Matthew captured Jesus' words about this as well:

This is how I want you to conduct yourself in these matters. If you enter your place of worship and, about to make an offering, you suddenly remember a grudge a friend has against you, abandon your offering, leave immediately, go to this friend and make things right. Then and only then, come back and work things out with God. (Matthew 5:23-24, MSG)

A careful reading of this text reveals something which, on the surface, may easily be overlooked. The cross has both vertical and horizontal beams. One reaches upward to God, the other outward to our fellow man. The *outward* relationship is so important that its rupture can short circuit fellowship in the *upward* relationship.

Not only is this true in reality with God, but in the perception of others. You can't be an authentic vessel of God's love if you can't love and forgive others. Breaches in human relationships invalidate our witness and nullify its veracity. People can sense when something's wrong. Joy cannot flow through the same pipe where bitterness, resentment, and unforgiveness flow. People may not see what's in your heart, but they sense what's in your spirit.

Our fellowship with God and our fellowship with people are inseparably bound up in our joy and peace. Our credibility, or lack thereof, with those to whom the joy should flow is at stake, and at so great a price.

You can't be right with God and *not* be right with your brother, any more than you can be right with your brother and *not* be right with God. One cross. Two beams.

But read it again. It's easy to miss. Jesus didn't say, "If *you* have something against your brother, leave your gift and reconcile, then come and worship." He said, "If you are offering your gift at the altar and there remember that your brother has *something against you* . . ." (verse 23, NIV, emphasis added). Initiate the process, *even if you have nothing against the other person.*

So essential is it that whether having been wronged or having done wrong, *you still initiate the process of reconciliation.* God has committed unto us the ministry of reconciliation, and it starts with you.

How do you approach someone who is bitter toward you when you have nothing against that person? One of the best ways is by letter. Not e-mail but *snail* mail. Handwritten. Better still, do it in person.

Don't apologize for having done something wrong if you feel you haven't. *Apologize for the situation.* Let the person feel your heart and know you really mean it. Tell him you'll do anything and everything to resolve the breach in your relationship. Let her know you are sincere and really do care.

If your apology is not received, let it go. You've done all you can. Leave it with God and walk away. But continue to love and pray for the person. In your heart, *forgive* them for *not forgiving you.*

And remember: Never apologize for the same thing twice. You will only make matters worse. If they didn't hear you the first time, they won't hear you the second. The good news is most people will welcome a sincere attempt at reconciliation.

Grudges and resentment are game changers. Do all in your power to fix the relationship, even if the problem is not yours. After you've done all you can do, go your way and go in peace. Your testimony has not been compromised; it has been strengthened.

Jesus, too, was the innocent party. We rebelled against Him, sinned against Him, and turned our backs on Him. His offense in our relationship is nonexistent. And who sought whom to accept their forgiveness?

If it is possible, as far as it depends
on you, live at peace with everyone.
ROMANS 12:18 (NIV)

CHAPTER 48

BE AN ENCOURAGER

M oses desperately wanted to lead the Israelites into the Promised Land. God allowed him to *see* the land, but only Joshua to *enter* it. He told Moses,

> Go up to the top of Pisgah and look west and north and south and east. Look at the land with your own eyes, since you are not going to cross this Jordan. But commission Joshua, and encourage and strengthen him, for he will lead this people across and will cause them to inherit the land that you will see. (Deuteronomy 3:27-28, NIV, emphasis added)

The gift of encouragement is one of the more unidentified gifts in the body of Christ. The Bible calls it the gift of exhortation. And it may be exercised more in daily living than Sunday morning preaching.

The gift of exhortation is not necessarily a gift of preaching. Encouragement is the counselor's gift. Far beyond being simply advisors or analysts, good counselors encourage their clients to believe they actually *can* do what the counselor tells them they *should* do. Encouragers are secure enough to say, "I want you to be secure too." "I want you to be a winner." "You can do it!" They give away the confidence they themselves possess, and in the process become stronger. There's the Cross again!

You may have no idea whether or not people are in a time of need, but your encouraging word makes a deposit in their lives that will be there when they need it. "A man hath joy by the answer of his mouth: and a word spoken in due season, how good is it!" (Proverbs 15:23).

One of my deacons was prominent in the Houston judiciary. He has the gift of encouragement. Both my heart and my scrapbooks are filled with an uncounted number of handwritten notes he sent me through the years. They were all unexpected, all just at the right time. They are one of the great treasures of my pastorate.

Writing notes of encouragement takes time. Take it. It's important.

And it's so easy to do. How much effort does it take to say, "Good job!" "Nice going!" "Thanks so much." "You blessed me."

And how much of your time does it take? Two seconds, maybe three?

Encouragement doesn't have to be profound or even spoken. It can come in the form of an affirming nod, a firm handshake, a smile, or a pat on the back. For those who look up to you, it can make their day—and change their life. In times of bereavement, the greatest comfort we can offer another is not *what* we say but that *we were there*. A personal visit can mean everything.

Be an encourager. You'll both be better for it.

Negative people are little people. And they don't make it to the finish line. Positive people are big people: They make it. And they want someone else to make it too.

A word fitly spoken is like apples of gold in pictures of silver.
PROVERBS 25:11

BE A MENTOR

The apostle Paul was a master discipler. Young Timothy was never the same because Paul mentored him. And how many thousands and millions of us have been mentored because he mentored Timothy!

Perhaps easily as significant was the impact of two very special women. "When I call to remembrance the genuine faith that is in you, which dwelt first in your grandmother Lois and your mother Eunice, and I am persuaded is in you also" (2 Timothy 1:5, NKJV).

Whatever you do, do it well and pass it on.

Help some young up-and-comers avoid the pitfalls, step over the land mines, and not make the same mistakes you made. Perhaps you can help them graduate a little sooner than you did from good ol' University of Hard Knocks. You can help them accelerate the success of their work or their ministry by months and even years.

In each of my seminary classes, I identify a student who's "got it." We start with a casual lunch to get acquainted and proceed to a monthly mentoring session with three or four others for about a year in our home. I am blessed by what these men became and are becoming. They still call me from time to time, and I love it. Their journey grows, and so do their ministries.

Jesus poured Himself into twelve men who changed the world. Why not ask God to give you twelve men or women, perhaps one or two at a time. It will be a source of deep satisfaction to know you left a legacy of tomorrow's young leaders in every profession. "And the things that thou hast heard of me among many witnesses, the same commit thou to faithful men, who shall be able to teach others also" (2 Timothy 2:2).

And the beat goes on—and on.

Being an example and being a mentor are closely connected. The greatest compliment you may ever receive is to find that someone wants to be just like you.

Intentional mentoring, however, goes further, lasts longer, and accomplishes even more. If a young follower of Christ seeks you out and asks for your time, give it to them. But let it originate with you as well. That special person may be only an inch or two away. One day you'll look back and say, "I had a part," and smile.

The older women likewise, that they be reverent in behavior, not slanderers, not given to much wine, teachers of good things—that they admonish the young women to love their husbands, to love their children, to be discreet, chaste, homemakers, good, obedient to their own husbands, that the word of God may not be blasphemed.

TITUS 2:3-5 (NKJV)

CHAPTER 50

FUNCTION IN YOUR GIFTEDNESS

A spiritual gift is a God-given, sovereignly chosen, Holy Spirit–empowered capacity to do something Jesus did. The fruit of the Spirit creates the character of Jesus—what He was like. The gifts of the Spirit create the ministry of Jesus—what He did.

There are three categories of spiritual gifts:

1. *The gift of the gifted person.* The sense in which, while the individual *has* the gift, he or she *is* the gift.
2. *Sign gifts to unbelievers to validate the message where there is no written Word or the Word is not believed.* Healing, speaking in languages you do not know, casting out demons, performing miracles.
3. *Gifts to edify the body of Christ.* Mercy, faith, giving, preaching, teaching, encouragement, leadership, administration, service, hospitality, discernment, evangelism.

If you are not ministering in your giftedness, you will never be comfortable, let alone productive. King Saul dressed young David in his weighty armor to fight the giant Goliath. David was neither comfortable nor effective wearing Saul's armor. Rather he chose to use the gifts God had inherently given him—and won! *You can't walk in Saul's armor.* There is absolutely nothing to be embarrassed about in acknowledging, "I need to make a change." Some of God's most effective servants reappraised their gifts and changed jobs. Some of the best pitchers in baseball used to play first base.

During my ministry, I have made four major shifts, all in God's time:

- Worship leader to preacher
- Evangelist to pastor
- One church to another
- The pastorate to retirement

Through the years, my passion was preaching evangelistic crusades. Today it is mentoring young pastors and conducting capital campaigns. The obvious question then is "How do I know my spiritual gift?"

I have found two indicators of giftedness.

The first indicator is what comes naturally.

Who are you? How has God made you? What do you do? What comes naturally—teaching, coaching, singing? Our grandson Jonathan graduated from Regent College Seminary in Vancouver, British Columbia. Only after he discovered the joy of farming and became an agricultural missionary in Nicaragua could he say, "I've found my life's calling." I think he wishes he had gone to Texas A&M.

What is your passion? Fill in the blank. If I could do anything in the world, I'd like to _____.

Is farming your passion? Be a farmer. Are you a natural caregiver? You could run a medical clinic in the inner city, or be a nurse. And here's the good news. Whoever you are, whatever you do, when you're *just being you*, somewhere in the world the need for you exists in Christian ministry.

You can't imagine the opportunities in the kingdom—filmmaking, home building, sports ministries, biker ministries, or cowboy churches.

You name it, somewhere, somebody's doing it for Christ. Why did God make only thousands of preachers but millions of Christian laymen and laywomen? The value of Christian doctors and nurses, farmers and homemakers, carpenters and beauticians is immeasurable.

Do what you like. That's what He created you to do, not to be miserable in His service.

The second indicator of giftedness is what God blesses.

If you think you are called to be an architect and every building you design implodes, think again.

If you're operating in your giftedness, you will receive some degree of affirmation and your comfort level will be very, very high. This has certainly been true for me.

My gift is preaching, not counseling. I like preaching and it's the most natural thing I can do. I can't tell you the number of times people have come up to me after a sermon and said, "Your message today changed my life."

Counseling is another matter. I don't really like counseling. And I'm certainly no good at it. I can't remember when anyone ever came to me after a counseling session and said, "You changed my life."

Passion and production are two indicators of giftedness. It comes naturally—God blesses it. Reexamine your giftedness. If you have to make a move, make it. Make it joyfully and make it now. The best is yet to come!

I wish that all men were as I am.
But each man has his own gift from God;
one has this gift, another has that.
1 Corinthians 7:7 (NIV)

CHAPTER 51

DON'T CRITICIZE

Encouragers build up. Critics tear down. Being an encourager takes a bit of effort, some time, and some words—good words, lots of words. Being a critic takes no effort at all—nothing, nada. And not criticizing is easier than you think. Just *don't say it.* It may cross your *mind,* but it doesn't have to cross your *lips.*

> *It only takes a spark, remember, to set off a forest fire. A careless or wrongly placed word out of your mouth can do that. By our speech we can ruin the world, turn harmony to chaos, throw mud on a reputation, send the whole world up in smoke and go up in smoke with it, smoke right from the pit of hell.* (James 3:5-6, MSG)

Words are important.

It's sad and sorrowful to hear people cut down others with their words. How much more for Christians!

The Bible is clear: Words are the indicator of the heart. The mouth is the fruit; the heart is the root. "Keep thy heart with all diligence; for out of it are the issues of life" (Proverbs 4:23).

There's a little bit of Simon Peter in us all. He denied with an oath, "I do not know the man. And after a while came unto him they that stood by, and said to Peter, Surely thou also art one of them; for thy speech betrayeth thee" (Matthew 26:72-73).

162   WISDOM *for* LIFE

"I do not know the man." Peter got it wrong.

"Your accent gives you away." The young maiden got it right.

Across the years, I have observed a constant pattern in the critic. Seldom do we criticize someone we consider our equal or less. We usually criticize someone we consider to be *more than we are*—more important, more popular, more successful. And what is that but *jealousy.* We have an inherent jealousy toward those who do what we do, and do it better.

How can I satiate my feeling of inferiority and jealousy? Either one of two ways: I can improve myself, study more, work harder, and be more. Or I can take the easy way and simply cut the other person down to my size.

Criticism levels the playing field. Criticism makes me feel better about myself by making you feel less about yourself.

How sad! Particularly for a man or a woman of God. Is our call to *lift Him up* or to *lift ourselves up*?

It all keeps coming back to the Cross, doesn't it?

Through the years, I've found that critics also criticize in the other person what they most dislike about themselves. What *Joe* tells me about *Bill* tells me more about *Joe* than it does about *Bill.* When you listen to critics, really listen. *They will be telling you about themselves.*

We don't have to build our self-esteem this way. There's a better way.

- Celebrate who you are in Christ.
- Thank God for the success He has given *you.*
- Everyone is essential to the body of Christ. The less attractive parts are actually the most important.
- The way up is down—less of me, more of Him.
- Keep growing toward Christ-likeness—you'll like yourself better.

Real love always lifts up and never cuts down. And it's easy. A pat on the back takes less effort than a kick in the pants. And there will come a day when you'll need it yourself. The pat, not the kick! "A word spoken in due season, how good is it!" (Proverbs 15:23).

Criticism cuts down. Encouragement builds up.
Which will it be?

———————

Death and life are in the power of the tongue.
PROVERBS 18:21

Let the words of my mouth, and the
meditation of my heart, be acceptable in thy sight,
O LORD, my strength, and my redeemer.
PSALM 19:14

CHAPTER 52

BE THANKFUL

How could a truly thankful person ever be anything except a faithful person? Quit? No way. Not on Him! Stop thanking Him? Never. Stop serving Him? Not gonna happen. My service far outlasts my acclamations of thanks. Gratitude keeps it all in perspective. It's never about me; I owe it all to Him. It keeps ever in focus who *He* is.

I'm grateful my country has an annual day for thanksgiving but saddened we so easily forget to be thankful the other 364 days.

Why is it so hard to be thankful? Perhaps because the blessings of God are so *unrestrained*. Some so *unrecognized,* until later. Some so *unremembered*. Like children unwrapping Christmas presents, we let our excitement about each one quickly overshadow our gratitude for the last.

As a parent and grandparent, I can sometimes feel a little twinge when a bit of thanks is lost in the excitement of opening the next gift. God must feel the same way about us as we unwrap His endless stream of blessings.

No one on earth has more for which to be thankful than I. God's unrestrained blessings on my life are at once overwhelming and undeserved. How could I ever let Him down?

I never went to seminary and have always regretted that. Yet today I serve on the adjunct faculty of a great seminary.

And I'm thankful.

I never took a course in preaching, yet my books on preaching have been studied by many pastors.

And I'm thankful.

Though I had no previous experience, the First Southern Baptist Church of Del City, Oklahoma, took a chance and offered me my first pastorate. It was wonderful.

And I'm thankful

I never took a course in writing, yet I've written many books.

And I'm thankful.

Far from the greatest husband in the world, I have the most wonderful wife on earth. She is more beautiful today than when we married and the greatest treasure in my life. Indeed an "angel unaware."

And I'm thankful.

My children serve the Lord as pastor's wife, evangelist, and Bible teacher. My three adult grandchildren are serving Jesus Christ. Two have just graduated from seminary. One serves in Japan.

And I'm thankful.

Twelve years after retirement from the pastorate, I haven't yet had time to rock on the front porch. Busier than ever, I begin my thirteenth year with my best schedule yet. It's everything I *want* to do and nothing I *have* to do. Those days are gone forever.

And I'm thankful.

But best of all, I'm one day closer to home. The King is coming. The world is crumbling, but I've read the last chapter of the Book and *we win*! And I can't wait to see the King!

Dear Jesus,

There's no way I could thank You for all You've done for me — Your gentle touch, Your loving grace, Your power that set me free. Through all my days, in all my ways, I still stand amazed. With all my heart, I truly pray, "May Jesus Christ be praised." Jesus, sweet Jesus, it's all because of You.

My life so rich, my heart so full, Your Word forever true. I bow my

head and bend my knee and in my heart I say, "Your love divine, Your
hand in mine, we made it all the way."

Love,

Bro. John

My sincere prayer is that you will know the joy of a life blessed by
His special touch and be faithful to the end.

And I shall be thankful — very, very thankful.

And let the peace of God rule in your
hearts, to the which also ye are
called in one body; and be ye thankful.

COLOSSIANS 3:15

NOTES

1. Rudyard Kipling, *Rewards and Fairies* (Bel Air, CA: BiblioBazaar, 2007), 115.
2. John Newton, "Amazing Grace," 1779.
3. George Barna, *Revolution* (Carol Stream, IL: Tyndale, 2005), 33.
4. H. B. London Jr., *Pastors at Greater Risk* (Ventura, CA: Regal, 2003).
5. William Barclay, ed., *The Letter to the Romans* (Philadelphia: Westminster, 1955), 165.
6. William Barclay, *The Daily Study Bible, The Gospel of Matthew Volume 1* (Philadelphia: Westminster, 1958), 166.
7. Kathy Antoniotti, "Mail Carrier Letters in Lifesaving," *The Houston Chronicle*, Section A, Page 2; July 16, 2010.
8. Tracy M. Sumner, ed., *The Essential Works of Andrew Murray* (Uhrichsville, OH: Barbour Publishing, 2008), 1176. Used by permission.
9. Charles Austin Miles, "In the Garden," 1912.
10. Barclay, *Daily Study Bible*, 142.

About the Author

JOHN BISAGNO is pastor emeritus of the 25,000-member First Baptist Church of Houston. He is the author of thirty books, including the best seller *The Power of Positive Praying*. Often called the pastor's pastor, he served as the president of the Southern Baptist Pastors' Conference. Dr. Bisagno has received three honorary doctoral degrees and serves on the adjunct faculty of Southwestern Baptist Theological Seminary, Houston, Texas.

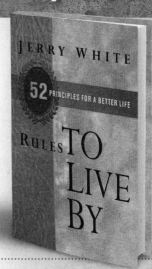

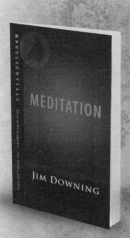